OUT
OF
GOD'S
CLOSET

This Priest Psychologist
Chooses **Friendly** Atheism

by
STEPHEN FREDERICK UHL

Golden Rule Publishers,
13401 Rancho Vistoso Blvd., #174
Oro Valley, AZ 85755

Out of God's Closet (ISBN: 9780979316937)
Originally *Imagine No Superstition* (ISBN: 9780979316906)
Published by
Golden Rule Publishers
13401 Rancho Vistoso Blvd., Unit 174
Oro Valley, Arizona 85755

author@OutOfGodsCloset.com
www.OutOfGodsCloset.com

Library of Congress Control Number: 2009902867

Cover by George Wheeler

Third Printing April 2009

Printed in the United States of America

Publishers Express Press
200 W. 5th Street So.
Ladysmith, WI 54848
pubexpress@centurytel.net
1-800-255-9929

10 9 8 7 6 5 4 3

Audio version of *Out of God's Closet*
read by the author,
No Gods, No Guilt, ISBN 9780979316920,
is a CD in MP3 format, 6.25 hours listening time.
Order directly from Golden Rule Publishers
www.NoGodsNoGuilt.com

DEDICATION

TO

BARACK OBAMA

who understands the full meaning of
our original American motto:

"E pluribus, unum"

"Out of many, we are one"

To make a friend
BE A FRIEND

I MET A FRIENDLY ATHEIST TODAY

    I know 'atheists are bad people' some say.

But this nice person was really good for me

    and helped me drop a childish fantasy.

Atheists I know now are not all bad;

    I hope that makes no one sad,

for here and now I enjoy this life more;

    their New Golden Rule helps my spirit soar,

for now that I know this life's no rehearsal,

    with mutual help we manage every reversal.

Dear Reader:

Do you ever wonder: ? ? ?

Why do innocent children die of leukemia or other diseases?

Who is in charge when a tsunami kills thousands of people?

Did U.S. guilt merit the terrorist attacks on 9/11/01?

Why do abortion clinics get bombed by religious believers?

Should we tolerate all faiths no matter how extreme?

Do I really need to believe most of what preachers preach?

Am I cynical when I fear praying preachers may be preying?

Can atheists, agnostics, freethinkers live good moral lives?

Are my dead loved ones gone forever?

Can I really go to a heaven of glory and pleasure forever?

Can I really go to a hell of shame and pain forever?

When, if ever, does the end justify the means?

When I was a little boy, a very little boy, **I learned** that I would go to heaven and be very happy: **if I obeyed** my mother and father; **if I loved** Jesus, the son of a special virgin; **if I believed** in the one God the Trinity of the Father, the Son and the Holy Ghost; **if I did not** eat meat on Friday; if I attended Mass on Sunday. I also learned very young that if I deliberately failed in any of these I would burn in an awful hell of punishment forever.

At this early impressionable time I learned that, while my oldest brother was destined to take over the family farm, I was definitely assigned to become the family priest. **My devout Catholic Mother taught me so!** Naturally, I believed it. And since I really believed it, I did it.

During the first nine of the eleven years when I was a young Catholic priest, I was a sincere believer. I effectively taught the same lessons of fear, guilt and prejudice that were handed down to me through other priests and family traditions. During those nine years, I created (and absolved) a lot of guilt and fear among believers. But a nearly fatal auto accident shook the very foundation of my faith.

As a retired psychologist, I am now enjoying mopping up some of the superstitious mess I contributed to as a naive young priest. It feels great to help readers see that the time to be happy is now, the place to be happy is here, and the way to be happy is to make others so.

Since I do as I believe, I write and speak now so that we all may enjoy being one planetary family, so that our joy may be as full as humanly possible.

This book was almost titled "The Book of Tolerance." While writing it, I realized that, even with my extensive education, I had gotten into my 30s before unlearning some traditional lessons of childhood. It's much easier to become tolerant of the believers of different belief systems when we realize how and why different individuals develop, learn and unlearn at different rates. It's not easy to let new knowledge replace the ingrained, imprinted old prejudices of childhood faith and superstition.

The following TABLE OF CONTENTS

shows you (after the short autobiographical Chapter One) a very quick overview of an exciting journey to secure freedom and joy that can be yours. When you, Dear Reader, get to the end of that journey I hope you will find it easy to enjoy the here and now as you enjoy helping others realize that the way to be happy is to make others so. I am confident that you will then find it easy to agree with that great orator, Robert Green Ingersoll:

"The time to be happy is now.
The place to be happy is here.
The way to be happy is to make others so."

The Author
February 2009

CONTENTS

INTRODUCTION

This book began as an intimate letter to my thirty-one nieces and nephews. I had just learned that I had prostate cancer, and I thought I didn't have long to live. My nieces and nephews were spread all over the continent, and I had not kept up to date with them very well. I did know that the group of thirty-one, along with their spouses and children, was a widely varied group, each individual and each family developing at its own unique pace.

As that intended letter progressed, I realized that many others might enjoy what I had to say. Meantime, my good urologist and I got control of the cancer, so I no longer thought I was staring at imminent death. Then the planned letter to relatives evolved into this book directed to a much wider readership. After all, I have been in the intimate family closets of a lot of families, both in the sacramental confessional and in the psychologist's office. Nevertheless, this book is by no means for everyone.

If you are perfectly happy and secure, you don't need this book. If you lack a sense of humor, don't bother trying to enjoy this book. If you lack a high school education, don't try to understand this book. If you are a highbrow scholar or university professor looking for formal and deep research, you will be disappointed. This book is for people who would like to find ways to be more tolerant of themselves and others. It is for people with some doubts and questions about how to confidently reconcile old family customs, ethics, and belief systems with twenty-first century knowledge and insights.

There is a war going on. Sometimes it is a hidden war within individuals fighting guilt and doubts; sometimes it's a war between groups that cannot tolerate one another. Way back in 1957, when

I was still a Catholic priest, I fought very differently in this war than I fight today. I hope this little book will help you reduce any personal conflict between family or ethnic traditions from the past and your desire to enjoy life fully in the present.

Many enemies of human joy are sincerely trying to undermine our free pursuit of happiness. They try to intimidate us and turn us away from a free and joyful modern life. They encourage us to bow and scrape and cower in fear and guilt. They would have us close our minds to a lot of liberty and pursuit of happiness, especially when such pursuit challenges their own traditions.

In my younger days, I myself unwittingly, but sincerely, helped intimidate many Americans on their way to happiness. I was a Roman Catholic priest for eleven years. During most of those years I worked hard to convert non-Catholics to become Catholics and to convince Catholics to work harder to live more perfectly in God's good graces. In my sermons, I used all of my powers of persuasion to show my audiences that they had better believe and do as good Christians of the gospel or they would go to a hell of suffering without God's grace.

In those early years of my priesthood, I believed strongly and deeply, so I lived and preached sincerely and heartily. Eight to ten years later, during an extended period of internal conflict, I studied, discussed, observed, argued, and consulted enough to become convinced that I may have been wrong for many years. I will share more details of this doubt-filled period a bit later.

Now in the autumn of my life, I see how I can repair some of the mistakes I made in the early stages of my journey. I realize that I must get this message out, for I am now convinced that I misled many in those early years.

I wish it were adequate to simply apologize. It might make many feel better if I apologized for my errors. More than apologies and good feelings is needed. Far more! Oh, how easy it would be to say "I'm sorry for misleading so many, for depriving them of so much human grace and freedom." But that too easy way out is not nearly enough. Though that would be far easier than the responsible solution, I see clearly that the more adequate solution demands that I do not now shirk my reasonable responsibility.

When I was a young, energetic, enthusiastic Catholic priest, the credulous often listened to and believed me merely because I was a priest. Horrible thought now in my maturity! As a result, I feel driven to step out of a comfortable and peaceful retirement to re-state my message in a caring effort to repair the harm done decades ago.

As I try to repair old errors, I find I am uniquely qualified to address believers, non-believers, and the doubters in between: as a former faithful Catholic priest and theologian who sweated through an extended period of doubt on the way to becoming an experienced atheistic psychologist, I understand a lot of conflicts within and between believers, doubters, and non-believers. And I now appreciate the great value of tolerance more than at any time in my life.

I hope this humble effort of mine will help bring believers, doubters and non-believers to better understand one another and listen to one another so sincerely that they can become united in their common humanity. I know this is a far-out goal, some would say an impossible goal; I think differently.

I have two sincere wishes for you: (1) that by the time you finish this message you will be totally comfortable with your own personal philosophy of life; and (2) that you will enjoy a much deeper understanding of fellow human beings who think and perceive differently than you do. It is primarily because of our differing abilities and perceptions that we learn at such different rates. Note the old couple in the middle of church services: she leans over and whispers to him: "I just let a silent fart; what should I do?" And he answered, "Change your hearing aid battery."

Traditions are hard, often painful, to shuck off. Traditions became traditions because they offered value at some point in the past; many of them still have great value. Most of us learned bundles of traditions, prejudices, and dogmas when we were little and looking up to everyone. We learned these basic and deeply influential lessons before we had any rational ability to evaluate such traditions.

These lessons learned in our pre-rational days are the hardest ones to evaluate and perhaps unlearn. So, in our efforts to reduce the causes of tension and contribute to freedom and the pursuit of happiness, patience with each other and with yourself is a must; we all learn and unlearn at our own speeds. I was a very slow un-learner of many of the impressive lessons of defenseless childhood. Sometimes we make mistakes because we behave like docile sheep, and sometimes we goof up because we act like stubborn mules. The practical challenge is to identify which tendency might be slowing our progress. Time after time we will need tolerance of our own foibles or doubts as well as those of others.

The first chapter of this book is the only one that is very autobiographical. This chapter will make it easier for us to travel an exciting journey together. You already know who you are; it will be more comfortable to also know who your traveling companion is.

We will then explore some of the main psychological reasons why most people feel there is a God. Philosophical proof of God's existence is then dealt with in Chapter Three. This, accompanied by biblical examples, leads to the conclusion that human reason alone can neither prove nor disprove God's existence. Intellectual agnosticism readily follows, but that, too, turns out to be less than satisfactory. The struggling agnostic finds instances of faith-based damage to society in Chapter Four.

By the time we get to Chapter Five, you will be more comfortable dealing with guilt and responsibility. "No guilt, no shame, no blame, just responsibility" will then make sense to you. The next chapter highlights several societal extremes that may result from too much credulity. After a brief chapter on "humility" (not lowliness), it becomes easier to understand how a natural person can relish life deeply and help others do the same. Chapters Eight and Nine show some of the many advantages of a purely natural life. Such a life promotes profound respect for each other while making it easier to observe The (Revised) Golden Rule as well as the First Amendment to the Constitution. The final Chapter, "Ten Commandments for the Twenty-first Century," encapsulates the book's central lessons.

I will seldom (almost never!) ask you to wade through formal or scholarly research anywhere in this book; I have already spent perhaps too much of my life on such matters. Most of the time I will simply share with you the practical lessons and insights gleaned from my experiences, memories, and observations. Please excuse me if this seems insufficient. As a caring person, I want you to become as comfortable with the practical conclusions you finally reach as I have become as I approach the end of my life. I hope you will become totally comfortable in knowing when to trust and when to verify, when to accept and when to reject, when to be more like the sheep and when to be more like the mule.

First, though, let's take a very brief look at the early, pre-determined part of my checkered life.

ONE

THE CHOSEN ONE

A SPECIAL ONE AMONG NINE

On a very hot summer night, in the depression year 1930, I was born in the same farmhouse bed as my five oldest siblings. That same bed would also witness the stage entrance of my three youngest brothers. Count 'em—nine kids! So would you guess this was a Catholic family?

Poor dad, he saw four daughters come into his life before he saw a son who could be designated to take over the farm. As the second son, mom pointed me toward the altar. So you might say I had a very early vocation to the priesthood; I cannot recall any childhood time when I was not going to be a priest. The large family that mom herself came from had already furnished several priests and monsignors to the church. Mom was anxious to make her own contribution through me.

When I was just a little boy, I was treated especially well. When mom gave me the golden brown crust of a still hot, freshly baked loaf of bread, or if she defended me in an argument with siblings, I savored her approval. It became clear to me later in childhood that I was mom's favorite. She was a fervent Catholic, and it was I, her child with the supernatural destiny, that was her chosen one.

My mom would have fit in very well with the following four ladies having coffee and boasting of the prowess of their sons. The first Catholic woman tells her friends, "My son is a priest. When he walks into a room, everyone calls him 'Father'." The second Catholic woman chirps, "My son is a bishop. Whenever he walks into a room, the people call him 'Your Grace'." This third Catholic lady says, "My son is a cardinal. Whenever he walks into a room, people say 'Your Eminence'." As the fourth Catholic woman silently sips her coffee, the first three women give her this subtle, "Well...?" So she responds, "My son is a gorgeous, 6' 2" hard bodied stripper. When he walks into a room, people say, "Oh, my God...."

Mom motivated me to work hard in school, and this paid me very good intellectual dividends. Thanks especially to mom's efforts, I developed a love for learning that I trust will never die until I do. I did disappoint her, however, when I flunked first grade. My teacher, Aunt Loretta, had told mother it would be better for me to start first grade at six. But mother just knew I could handle it at age five. She wanted me to move along as quickly as possible academically. Well, Aunt Loretta had her own teacher's ideas, and she made her point by flunking me so that I repeated first grade at age six.

During grade school, I enjoyed being an altar boy, because I believed that the religious ceremonies brought me to God. At the same time, I enjoyed strutting my liturgical stuff in the sanctuary before my mom and the rest of the parishioners. In my boyhood, we considered the priests to be special and thought they deserved the greatest respect. There was no hint of pedophilia from our priests at Saint Michael's church. (Much later I learned of some alcohol abuse and nocturnal extra-celibate activities, but never pedophilia.)

So the priesthood was a very attractive goal for me at the ripe old age of 14 in spite of a couple of puppy-love crushes that did not follow me to the seminary. I really did believe without reservation that I was destined to be of special service to God and his church.

SEMINARY

When this young farmer's son entered the boarding seminary at Saint Meinrad, Indiana, I was impressed to the point of being overwhelmed. The size of the buildings, the numbers of classmates and new friends, and the busyness of the schedule added up to a challenging thrill for me. I followed the strict rules, studied and played hard, and enjoyed the exciting growth of it all.

I even enjoyed the institutional cooking that some of the city kids complained about. Being from a large and poor family, I was already accustomed to sharing with others and appreciating the food that was available. I was less accustomed to luxuries than were some of my classmates. Homesickness quickly reduced the number of our freshman classmates. Through the coming six years (minor seminary), the young ladies naturally attracted many others to abandon the long trek to the altar and ordination. I myself fought through and sublimated those natural attractions of adolescence which were then included in "temptations of the flesh."

I vividly remember the main point of Father Adelbert's annual June sermon to us as our Spiritual Director: "You can go home for this summer vacation, and you can go out with girls if you want to; that's O.K. If you really want to go out with girls, go ahead and do so; just don't come back!" Of course, a lot did not come back. I sublimated those natural drives while wearing out a lot of tennis shoes as a local championship handball player.

After two years of college, we came to what we called "the parting of the ways." The six-year minor seminary chapter closed as the next chapter of six years of major seminary studies opened.

Some of the classmates, most really good friends by this time, continued at the Saint Meinrad major seminary preparing for service either in the parishes or going to the Benedictine monastery at Saint Meinrad. Philosophy and theology became the principal studies during these six years.

MARMION ABBEY AND MARMION MILITARY ACADEMY

A few of us parted further from our fond Saint Meinrad roots and went into the Benedictine monastery at Aurora, Illinois, for our major seminary studies. I chose this option for a couple of specific reasons. The head of this young monastery was Abbot Gerald Benkert, former rector of the minor seminary at Saint Meinrad. I knew and admired him as a very intelligent man; and I knew this new monastery would need manpower to run their high school, Marmion Military Academy. I looked forward to teaching at the Academy.

At Marmion Abbey we lived a full time monastic life without vacations or frequent trips home; we had the monastery as our new and "unworldly" home. We learned to humble ourselves, leave all the world and family, give up property and pleasures, and follow Christ. This harsh lifestyle stressed humility, lowliness, personal unworthiness, and guilt, especially during the first year, the novitiate year.

Our hard-of-hearing and not-too-smart novice master demanded and achieved a lot of subjugation. I can still remember his giving me a penance merely for my insisting that "Why?" was one of the most important questions a human can ask. He probably should have done us both the favor of expelling me then. Besides being a pain in his intellectual backside, I labored without pay (along with the other novices) at mopping the floors, cleaning the toilets and tilling the monastery farm.

This lifestyle demanded a lot of sublimation. I lived it fully with total and undoubting faith and credulity in its merits. At the end of the novice year, I deliberately made the five vows of the Benedictine monastic system: (1) poverty (practically no personal property); (2) chastity (no sex); (3) obedience (no independent personal authority); (4) conversion of morals (a catch-all); and, (5) stability (no roaming off the monastery grounds without permission). And you thought you had it tough? Hey, full and blind faith can be pretty blinding. But it drove me to embrace the system completely.

Having survived the humiliating novitiate year, the remaining five years of my major seminary studies of mostly philosophy and theology went well. I knew how to study, get along, and sublimate passionate temptations, while keeping busy with a lot of formal and informal praying. I must admit, however, that I did a lot of sleeping during the repetitive droning of the many psalms and prayers of Matins. These very long "morning prayers" that we said at night often bored this tired monk into the arms of Morpheus by their deadly daily, weekly, and annual repetitiveness.

All these prayers, studies, and humiliations, eventually led to the altar and ordination to the priesthood in 1956. What a high this produced! I truly believed I could now absolve sinners of guilt that would otherwise damn them, and I believed I had the special power to change bread and wine into the body and blood of Jesus Christ. This was very heady stuff for the true believer, which I was. Of course, mom rode high above cloud nine when I got ordained; she had contributed a son to the service of the Church. And neither she nor anyone else could have foreseen the developments of the next eleven years.

HIGHER THEOLOGICAL STUDIES

After ordination to the priesthood, Abbot Gerald asked if I would like to pursue higher theological studies. He offered to send me to Catholic University of America in Washington, D.C., where he himself had earned a Ph.D. in philosophy *summa cum laude*. His offer of such a challenge and honor thrilled me, and I jumped at it.

At Catholic University, I studied and partied with intellectually bright priests and professors from all over the Christian world.

We learned more about Christian archeology, Church history, the origins and developments of morals and dogmas of the Christian Church than we would ever need to know in real life. However, I did not consider it useless at the time. I even went along with the general attitude prevailing at the university which held that working clergy in pastorates were "really quite innocent of theology." (This still appears to be mostly true.)

In spite of seeing the historical, political, and natural developmental warts of the Church, I still believed in the supernatural, the divine character and foundation of that dogmatic organization. I returned to Marmion Abbey with the S.T.L. (*Sacrae Theologiae Licentia*), the license to teach theology in pontifical universities.

Abbot Gerald was pleased. I am confident that if I had played my cards as expected I would have been his nominee to become his successor. But a funny thing happened on the way to the Abbot's throne.

THE ROAD TO AGNOSTICISM

I enjoyed most of the next ten years teaching religion, mathematics, and counseling at Marmion Military Academy. During the week, I worked with the high school youngsters. On weekends I engaged in pastoral work in a variety of northern Illinois parishes. I believed that I was doing the will of God and that helping others do the same would eventually win heaven for me as well as for those I thought I was helping. I gave no reason to anyone to doubt the sincerity of my faith. But the outcome of this varied decade of learning and growth surprised me and disappointed many friends and family who had more conventional expectations of me.

At about 34 years of age, a snag developed. One morning during private meditation in the abbey chapel, I chose to analyze the intellectual proofs of God's existence. I had done this many times before without meaningful incident. On this fateful morning in 1964, I had an insight that struck me perhaps as forcefully as the reported "lightning bolt" that struck Paul of Tarsus from his high horse. It wasn't really that exaggerated, of course, but it was a deeper insight into this matter than I had ever admitted before.

I saw clearly how Saint Thomas' strongest proof fell short of proving God's existence; it was based on an unwarranted assumption. (I will deal much more fully with the inadequacy of Saint Thomas' causality proof in the next chapter.) Note that the Catholic Church taught dogmatically that pure reason, clear thinking, unaided by faith, could logically prove God's existence. That fateful insight into Saint Thomas' unwarranted assumption laid the foundation for personal upheaval while loosening the underpinnings of my faith in the Church and in the very existence of God.

Over the next two years, I would gradually develop from a strong believer who performed in a manner consistent with my beliefs into an agnostic who was no longer sure of the faith system I had learned so early and so thoroughly. Those two years included consultations with a wide variety of reputedly wise persons as well as tumultuous private meditations and internal arguments. These discussions and arguments convinced me that I no longer believed as a credulous child.

Outside of matters of faith, I had always taken pride in being logically and intellectually directed rather than emotionally driven. I had drunk my faith with my mother's milk. Now I faced a challenge I had never envisioned: how could I be true to my intellectual self while doubting mother's faith and the church I was so marked to serve? I continued to preach purely moral sermons. It was still comfortable for me to teach how to "love your neighbor as you love yourself." I simply avoided sermons on dogmatic matters of faith.

But horrible hypocrisy besieged me when I acted as though I believed what I said at mass as I pronounced those formerly awesome words of consecration: "This is my body...; this is my blood..." Though the long hypnotic spell of faith had been broken for me, I still needed to play the hypocrite for several months in early 1967, so I could end the academic year's duties responsibly and without public scandal. Once I had admitted to becoming a sincere agnostic, I had to divorce myself from the monastery, a wealth of good friends, the Church, and religion. This divorce process, like most divorces, was not as simple and painless as it might have been.

FINAL DIVORCE FROM MARMION AND THE CHURCH

In June 1967, I left my monastic family and friends at Marmion. Many of the friends are still unforgettable. After all, I had lived closely with most of this group of men for 17 years. The attitude of Abbot Gerald, an intelligent gentleman to the end, was rather touching. Shortly after I had signed his proffered form promising "not to sue" for whatever cause, he surprised me. Without any hint or suggestion from me, he opened his office safe and handed me an impressive amount of cash to help me get started in the real world. Frankly, I have always felt that this bright Ph.D. *summa cum laude* would have jumped at the chance to follow me to independence and freedom if he had been 10 years younger and if he had not enjoyed so much organizational power and comfort. (I think the same is true of many Catholic bishops in powerful and cushy positions.)

Thanks to helpful friends, I really was not nearly as needy as Abbot Gerald had feared. Besides, as an experienced teacher with more than a master's degree, I had already signed an attractive contract with an outstanding suburban school district. I never went hungry.

I did have some lonely times. In fact, I visited Marmion to see old friends several times. However, I sensed an underlying discomfort in some of the monks and clear disapproval in others, so I soon stopped those trips from Des Plaines to Aurora, Illinois. Besides, my work and increasing social interests gradually filled my life; this made the final steps of my divorce from Marmion less painful than the initial ones.

MARRIAGE

On the Winter Solstice of 1968, I married another master's level teacher in our Illinois Public High School District 214. We shared deep interests in helping youngsters get the best possible start in life. As mature adults, we both enjoyed the fruits of our middle class backgrounds. And we were both agnostic regarding supernatural matters.

Now that I had married a working woman, I could afford to get the doctorate and become the psychologist I had long wanted to become. On the way to the Ph.D. at Loyola University of Chicago, I became a certified school psychologist. My doctoral dissertation examined how aspects of parents' communication skills influenced their fifth-graders' self-esteem and achievement levels. In addition, I became certified as an Illinois Public School Administrator (K-12), though I had no plans to ever become a school principal or superintendent. (Does it appear I may have studied too much?)

Perhaps I subconsciously feared that I would later fail in the private practice of psychology. In any event, after receiving the doctorate in 1975, I continued to work as a school psychologist for a year while beginning my private psychological practice.

PRIVATE PRACTICE OF PSYCHOLOGY

As I began building my clientele in 1976, I was a confirmed agnostic in a very Christian Chicago suburban area. It was truly amazing how often my clients had problems of conflict between their faith and their reasonable common sense. The guilt that resulted was sometimes crushing for the conscientious. Though at times stressful for me, I relished the work with a wide variety of private clients. I oriented my therapy to helping clients become self-responsible in dealing with perceived problems and pleasures. I often used hypnosis, which is concentrated attention accompanied by deep relaxation, to speed this growth process along. I thrilled to see clients crippled by guilt get up and walk tall, now joyfully guilt-free and self-responsible after shucking off old fears and superstitions.

For instance, one conscientious young mother of three, already feeling overwhelmed by maternal demands, definitely did not want more children. As a Catholic forbidden to use birth control, how could she meet her husband's needs and diminish his anger and frustration? Most Catholics now find the reasonable answer and simply ignore the pope and his prohibition of responsible birth control. That answer comes easily for the objective thinker, but to the Catholic believer back then there seemed to be no very satisfactory or guilt-free answer.

The joy that resulted from helping these conflicted spirits blossom into free, self-responsible adults far exceeded any joy that resulted from telling a confessing sinner "I absolve you in the name of the Father and of the Son and of the Holy Ghost" in the Catholic confessional booth. I realized the superstitious sinner would likely return next week, next month, or next year with the same list of sins.

INVITATION TO AN EXCITING JOURNEY

I have included this very brief summary of my checkered life to help you understand how my perspective developed. The following thoughts may challenge and excite you. Through the coming pages, I hope we can all stretch tall enough to see beyond our current horizons, think critically for ourselves, and see further than we can see now. But let's always remain dedicated to tolerance: I will tolerate you if you can tolerate me.

In the following chapter, we should come to a fuller appreciation of how and why most people believe or feel the need to believe there is a God or something beyond nature.

―――

SEQUITUR/NON SEQUITUR—HALLELUJAH

A man bought a donkey from a preacher. The preacher told the man that this donkey had been trained in a very unique way, (being the donkey of a preacher). The only way to make the donkey go is to say "Hallelujah!" The only way to make the donkey stop is to say "Amen!"

The man was pleased with his purchase and immediately got on the animal to try out the preacher's instructions. "Hallelujah!" shouted the man. The donkey began to trot. "Amen!" shouted the man. The donkey stopped immediately.

"This is great!" said the man. With a "Hallelujah!" he rode off very proud of his new purchase.

The man traveled for a long time through some mountains. Soon he was heading towards a cliff. He could not remember the word to make the donkey stop. "Stop," said the man. "Halt!" he cried. The donkey just kept going. "Oh, no ... Bible... Church!... Please stop!!" shouted the man. The donkey just began to trot faster. He was getting closer and closer to the cliff edge. Finally, in desperation, the man said a prayer... "Please, dear Lord, please make this donkey stop before I go off the end of this mountain. In Jesus name, AMEN."

The donkey came to an abrupt stop just one step from the edge of the cliff.

"HALLELUJAH!" shouted the man...

TWO

WHY MOST PEOPLE BELIEVE IN GOD

In September 2005 a huge category five hurricane Rita was bearing down on the gulf shores of Texas. The desperately frightened Governor of Texas had over a million people make their exodus inland. And after the historically dire warnings to these anxious citizens, the good governor told them to "say a prayer for Texas."

One of our oldest defense mechanisms, in common use yet today, is wishful thinking. This is the belief that wishing can somehow change reality or make things happen. A simple dictionary definition of wishful thinking is "the attribution of reality to what one wishes to be true and the tenuous justification of what one wants to believe." Of course, wishes do sometimes become reality for two reasons: first, when we are directly or personally responsible for the wished-for result, we likely take at least some steps to achieve it; likewise, even when we are not directly responsible for the wished-for results, good things can and do happen. For example, if we are wounded or sick, Mother Nature is so bountiful that we often heal or get well as we wished, though consciously we did nothing but wish for that good result.

Both situations reinforce our belief in our wishing; our wishes are intermittently fulfilled as they do sometimes come true. Such intermittent reinforcement is the strongest kind of psychological reinforcement. This helps explain why wishful thinking is so common. The associative thinker very easily concludes: "I wished for it, therefore it happened." *"Post hoc, ergo propter hoc"* (after the act, therefore because of the act) is only sometimes true. There is no reliable connection between the wishful thinking and the outcome even though a strong connection is frequently perceived by the wisher. The same holds for prayer.

WISHFUL THINKING, PRAYER AND HYPNOSIS

Prayer is commonly an act of wishful thinking. And since prayer is frequently more hypnogenic than simple wishful thinking, prayer can take on an added level of effectiveness. When I say that prayer works sometimes, I really mean it. Prayer often works for the wishing believer who is doing the praying. Reliable objective research has shown clearly that prayers offered by others for someone's improvement without that person's knowledge have no effect on that person at all. However, when the believer prays for his own wishes to come true, they are more likely to come true than if he had not prayed. This is because of the hypnotic character of prayer.

In my psychological practice, I often used hypnosis, which is similar to modern meditation, in order to help my patients achieve their goals. I frequently dubbed hypnosis "meditation in high gear." It is a most powerful and effective tool; it helps a person relax deeply, concentrate, and access his own personal powers. In fact, hundreds of my clients amazed themselves when they quit smoking, generally without withdrawal effects, after only one session of individual hypnosis.

The hypnotized or meditating person is often surprised at his newly discovered strength and capabilities. Before being hypnotized he thought himself incapable of doing what he wanted or achieving what he needed for happiness; after hypnosis he sees more clearly his own potential, his own ability to achieve his goals. Once the hypnotized patient realized the magnitude of his own internal power, he rapidly progressed toward mental health and independence. For example, he now moves from the attitude of 'I cannot quit smoking' to the conviction that 'I can quit smoking.'

Now prayer that is effective can be appropriately called self-hypnosis. It helps the praying person relax and focus his attention and wishes. In so doing, the concentrating, praying person hypnotizes himself and convinces himself that his goal is attainable. Then, with the resulting increase in confidence, the hopeful praying subject sometimes goes on to achieve his desired goal. Thus the praying subject is successful precisely as the hypnotized subject is successful: both realize and use power beyond what they had previously thought possible.

Even though prayer does not work because of a Higher Power's power, it is easy to see how it strengthens the faith of the wishful thinking believer. Jesus Christ may have realized this informally when he commanded his followers not to pray publicly like the hypocrites but secretly or privately (Matthew 6:5-6). Private prayer is much more effective (for non-political purposes) than public prayer, because personal concentration and meditative insights are much more likely in private than in public.

Understand how the self-hypnosis of prayer is sometimes so effective for the praying believer. His achievement beyond what he had thought himself capable of positively reinforces his act of self-hypnotic praying. This greater-than-expected personal achievement is intermittent, so it strongly reinforces the faith of the praying person. Therefore, he becomes more convinced of the power of prayer while thinking that prayer gets its power from God rather than from within himself. He prayed to his God; he got greater-than-expected results. Therefore, he attributes the results to God's help; *post hoc, ergo propter hoc.*

Further, the more convinced the praying person becomes of the power of prayer, the better he becomes at hypnotizing himself, so the more effective his self-hypnotic prayer becomes. Now you can understand how it is feasible for a person who does not understand hypnosis to attribute a supernatural power to prayer. Such reinforcement is a strong argument for millions to believe in a Higher Power. For the person who understands hypnosis, however, prayer works, not because some God changed his eternally changeless divine mind, but because the self-hypnotizing subject changed his own mind and increased his own personal effectiveness.

Even public prayer does actually have some desired effect at times. Most individuals are somewhat swayed by what the crowd seems to believe. The listening crowd is helped toward hypnosis by the repetitions or the soothing or authoritative voice of the preacher or politician. This believing crowd, led in prayer by an articulate leader, grows in unity until all or most in the crowd say "Amen" to the same thing. As the preacher or group leader uses his hypnotic power, even unwittingly, he can readily strengthen the crowd's self-reinforcing belief and help it reach some degree of mass hypnosis or even mass hysteria. (Churchill, Hitler, Franklin D. Roosevelt, and many popular evangelical preachers have been masterful crafters of the convictions of crowds.)

The power (for good or ill) that becomes obvious here is not a power above nature; it is the self-hypnotically induced power of increased conviction in individuals who earlier had been unconvinced of their power. This power is so great that it may be directed to repair a community, start a violent revolution or increase contributions to or votes for all kinds of causes.

INFLUENCE OF TWO KINDS OF CROWDS—
HISTORICAL AND CURRENT

Now this influence of the crowd can grow down through the years (longitudinal, historical), or the influence can come from the contemporary crowd (latitudinal, current). The example above is latitudinal; like the ripples on a pond, the influence or power spreads and grows wider and wider as it engulfs more and more of the current crowd. Hearing and seeing the active crowd influences others to join in here and now.

On the other hand, a longitudinal crowd is more like a river of influence flowing down through time. Examples might be a lasting dynasty, a royal family, a traditional association, a historic religion, a historic political party, or acceptors of a traditional myth. When a person joins a group or crowd, gang or sect, he gathers strength from and lends strength to the group. The more completely he embraces the beliefs and traditions of the longitudinal group, the more totally the group accepts him. He also draws further strength or conviction from the group. Thus, there is a self-reinforcing cycle of individual accepting group accepting individual accepting group, etc.

This mutual strengthening process in the traditional or longitudinal group, "history's crowd," is quite similar to the mutual reinforcement of the mass hypnosis process in the latitudinal group or "today's crowd" described earlier. Group hypnosis enhances the strength of individuals in "today's crowd" as the individual self-hypnotizing members strengthen the growing crowd itself. The same applies to the river of "history's crowd"—the believers of the past are believed by the current believer; he accepts their traditions, gains confidence and strength from those traditions, and so he adds his influence to strengthen the group that contributed to his strength.

Whether the crowd is longitudinal or latitudinal, the bigger it is, the easier it is to attract followers. Nothing succeeds like success especially in matters of opinion or belief in things that are beyond evidence. In numbers there is strength; and the fellowship feels good, so fellow-believers quite naturally strengthen one another. The result is that most people today still hold on to a plethora of traditions and beliefs of old. Critical thinking is needed to evaluate many of those customs and belief systems handed down from pre-scientific centuries.

SEQUITUR/NON SEQUITUR—HEALING THE SICK

Grandma and Grandpa were watching a healing service on television. The evangelist called to all who wanted to be healed to go to their television set, place one hand on the TV and the other hand on the body part where they wanted to be healed.

Grandma got up and slowly hobbled to the television set, placed her right hand on the set and her left hand on her arthritic shoulder that was causing her great pain. Then Grandpa got up, went to the TV, placed his right hand on the set and his left hand on his crotch.

Grandma scowled at him and said, "I guess you just don't get it; the purpose of doing this is to heal the sick, not raise the dead."

POWERFUL EFFECTIVENESS OF FEAR AND GREED

Another understandable reason so many believe in God and the good of religion is religion's easy use of the combination of fear and greed. These emotions of fear and greed are two of the most basic and powerful human motivators; they are so powerful, in fact, that they can readily override reason's control with their "stick and carrot" type of drive. Have you ever made a mistake? Then did you feel guilty or inadequate? And finally, did you feel better when you believed

God lovingly forgave you and blessed you with his saving grace? The fear and greed showing here are the underpinnings of a lot of divine faith.

You tend to "listen up" when a figure of authority says, "O you weak and wayward, born in sin, give to the poor; give to my good cause and you will get your reward in heaven. I, your pastor, offer you a great investment program! Give me the fruits of your labor; trust me to use your money productively; trust me to do God's will; I am your representative, priest or mullah before God. And you get in return? Eternal, endless, perfect happiness in heaven, I promise. Believe me; trust me to keep you from the hell you may deserve on your own without my supernatural help."

RELIGION'S ADDICTIVE COMBINATION OF FEAR AND GREED

I remember well responding to such messages, so I readily understand how the credulous person now becomes terrified and feels very inadequate. Sympathize with his fear and insecurity as he says to himself: "What if the preacher is right? He seems so sure of his message! Tradition and my mom support him. Maybe I am inadequate to fight my own battles and repair my own mistakes. I sure don't want to miss out on the great eternal deal the preacher is offering!" This circular or self-reinforcing system of terror and rewards (stick and carrot) has worked for centuries. Those two strong motivators, fear and greed, figure in here so strongly as to readily establish a self-sustaining cycle.

This self-sustaining stick and carrot cycle helps me understand why most people want to hold on to God or religion. From the days of pre-rational youth, nearly everyone can find reason for distrusting self; older family members, the culture, tradition, the minister, our own stupid mistakes and other authority figures repeatedly gave us reason to distrust our own judgment. For anyone lacking in self-confidence, it is easy to reach for the offered support of redemptive religion, becoming as a little child and believing another more than oneself. Christ is quoted as having said that unless you become as little children you cannot enter the kingdom of heaven. The believer feels strong and confident while depending on this superhuman strength, which can motivate him to try to find yet more strength in religion.

The psychological and practical dynamic is very simple and effective. As in classical brainwashing, the first step is to shake the self-confidence that the potential convert may have. Humble him; get him to fear that he is inadequate in himself. For the young and ill-educated, this first stage is usually quite easy. It allows the hearer to become credulous and say "yes," believing that the trainer, novice-master, or preacher is offering a deal that is superior to what this humbled or guilty one could achieve on his own. So now he jumps at the chance to invest his lowly self to get an eternal reward.

Greed now takes over as he sees he can get a lot for a little. Greed gets stronger as it feeds on itself; the new believer now trusts the salesman's attractive presentation so completely that he, as a caring person and as an insecure and greedy person, wants to become a salesman or pitch-man himself. This helps him to believe more securely in the promised reward that he now, as the new generation preacher, promises to others. The more believers he can influence to join the righteous, the stronger becomes his own faith. There is, indeed, strength in numbers.

Then a wonderful thing happens on the way to perfection and higher knowledge: the new convert, now a preaching, promising representative of God, experiences a new feeling of superiority and power, a much better feeling than what he experienced as a lowly wretch unworthy of grace. "I was weak, but now I am strong." The believer's faith grows stronger the more he preaches it, and so he preaches more enthusiastically, as I myself did. Pretty soon no one can convince him that he might be addicted to the newly found cheap power of being a representative of God with supernatural power.

When Moses couldn't get the Jews to listen to him as a merely human leader, what did he do? He greedily grabbed a power greater than himself and claimed to have almighty God on his side. The wayward Jews could readily disobey Moses as just a human leader, but when he assumed God's power, Moses really took charge. "When Moses went and told the people all the Lord's words and laws, they responded with one voice, 'Everything the LORD has said we will do.'" (Exodus 24:3) Cheap power, but very effective!

Is this use of cheap power, using greed and fear as it does, much different from the televangelist collecting money from the ignorant and poor who are truly afraid to miss out on cheap help in solving their very real problems? "Send in just $x.00 to help my poor, and I will pray to Almighty God to bless you. He will bless you infinitely (greed on both parts). And if you ignore the needs of the poor and my great, blessed, divine mission, be careful; you may be ignoring God, and if you ignore him, he may just ignore you for all eternity. Now touch your television screen, and I will send a prayer for you."

For the believing and insecure, this is powerful stuff; fear and greed work. This team of fear and greed drives a great deal of stock market investment activity; and it powers many more millions in their spiritual investment schemes. So they believe in God in great numbers.

RELIGIONS DO A LOT OF VERY GOOD THINGS

Yet another reason so many people choose to believe in religion and God is that religions and religious people really accomplish good works. Many thousands of volumes have been written to sanctify and magnify these good works by religions. These volumes continue to flow from the presses in an unending flood, so I will not add much to that already great volume of testimony.

Who could ignore the helpful works of mother Theresa, the Salvation Army, the YMCA, the YWCA, Catholic Charities, and some religious schools? Thousands of religious groups work daily to feed the hungry of body and mind. Such groups often help drive the drug pushers from their neighborhoods, bring hope to the hopeless, run schools and social service clubs of many kinds.

Religious schools often do a superior job of educating young-sters. These schools achieve good discipline (by whatever means) that is basic to efficient teaching and learning. Recognizing the benefits that religious efforts often contribute to society, it is commonly accepted that religion helps society more than it hurts it. This evident benefit of religion is yet another reason so many believe in God.

SEQUITUR/NON SEQUITUR—CATHOLIC MATH

Little Tommy (who was Jewish) was doing very badly in math. His parents had tried everything: tutors, specialists, counselors, everything they could think of. Finally, in a last ditch effort, they enrolled Tommy in the local Catholic school.

After the first day, little Tommy came home with a very serious look on his face. He didn't even kiss his mother. He went straight to his room and started studying. Books and papers were spread all over the room, and little Tommy was hard at work.

His mother was amazed. She called him to dinner, and, to her shock, the minute he was done he marched back to his room without a word; in no time he was back hitting the books. This went on for some time, day after day, while mother tried to understand what made all the difference.

Finally little Tommy brought his report card home. He quietly laid it on the table and went to his room and hit the books again. With great trepidation, his mom looked at the report card, and, to her surprise, Tommy got an "A" in math.

Mom could no longer hold her curiosity. She went to his room and said: "Son, whaaaat was it?? Was it the nuns?"

Little Tommy looked at her and shook his head, no.

"Well, then, was it the books, the discipline, the structure, the uniforms?? WHAT WAS IT?"

Little Tommy looked at her and said, "Well, on the first day of school, when I saw that guy nailed to the plus sign, I knew they weren't fooling around."

WOMEN ANOTHER CAUSE OF BELIEF IN GOD

Seeing the gross male chauvinism that has stood out in most historic religions, I have asked myself many times, why do more women believe in God and attend church than men? The answer is complex and has a great deal to do with pre-twenty-first century women's self-confidence and self-esteem.

Traditional male chauvinism in the Bible, Koran and Book of Mormon, following earlier pagan traditions, all assumed God to be male. Some religions have even worshipped God's phallus. Male priesthoods gave the cushy and powerful religious jobs to men, while women were left to serve in secondary roles if at all. Since the male priests represented a male God, chauvinism became institutionalized by history's longitudinal crowd. Scripture repeatedly tells women to be silent in church and to be subject to their husbands. The result in the past has been for women, officially and traditionally treated as inferiors, to consider themselves as inferior. If any fallacy is repeated often enough, it is eventually believed by many!

With low self-esteem resulting from abusive male chauvinism, it is harder for women to be self-confident and self-reliant. So, if chauvinistic society is abusive, dependent women can find strength by escaping into the supernatural. I can understand how a female victim of male chauvinism would readily resort to wishful thinking and tell herself: "There just has to be more fairness in the totality of life than this; I deserve better. I feel safer in the arms of Jesus; God will strengthen and reward me." (The deep religious faith of the abused black slaves in American history was another graphic demonstration of this escapist dynamic of wishful thinking. Though these poor slaves may not have been allowed to read, they were allowed their religion for the consolation, hope and strength they drew from it.) Women's lack of self-reliance based in male chauvinistic abuse has kept many of them seeking the strength and consolation of a Higher Power with promises of better things to come.

Thankfully, modern American women are shaking off much of the tyranny born of traditional chauvinism. Women are not currently typed "the weaker sex" in America nearly as readily as historically or as in more theocratic parts of the world. Evidence of growing female ego-strength continues to grow rapidly in this early part of the twenty-first century. However, if you go to church or study the pictures of Christian religious crowds, count the heads, yes, even in America, and you will see there is still quite a way to go. Certainly in religious circles, the equality of the sexes is not yet!

WOMEN ARE INFLUENTIAL TEACHERS

Nevertheless, it is difficult to over-estimate the power of women, especially powerful in their roles as mothers and teachers of the impressionable upcoming generation. They are one of the most powerful reasons so many people still feel they must believe or at least act religious or follow old ways. Mothers' values and beliefs make very deep impressions on their children. A big and common problem develops when mothers are not confident as to how to best raise or teach the children. Too often, in desperation, mothers lacking in self-reliance turn to confident-sounding dogmatic spiritual leaders for guidance. (Can you perhaps still remember your mother telling you that God would punish you if you did not obey her?) I personally shudder at the authoritarian advice I gave to mothers when I was still a celibate and naive young priest. Wow! Talk about the blind leading the blind!

"The hand that rocks the cradle rules the world" more effectively than even most mothers admit. One defensive young mother sent the following note by way of her son to his new kindergarten teacher: "Dear teacher, the opinions expressed by this child are not necessarily those of his mother." Oh? If mothers and teachers of the very young are self-confidently fact-based, their charges are likely to grow in fact-based self-confidence. If mothers and teachers of the very young are myth-based or superstitious, their charges are likely to grow in superstition-based credulity. Surely no one should feel guilty or ashamed that such lessons from pre-rational days are hard to unlearn. I was in my thirties when I got free of them. Patience, fearlessly free inquiry into anything factual and open discussions produce growth in understanding of reality.

The central concept of superstition as understood throughout this book is very close to the concept as defined by Webster: belief or practice resulting from ignorance, fear of the unknown, trust in magic or chance, or a false conception of causation.

I am confident that modern women are far less superstitious, less credulous and more self-confident than were their grandmothers. So this generation of mothers and teachers has better ego-strength and greater self-confidence than grandma had. I deeply appreciate observing the current rapid decrease in male chauvinism in America and the related increase in modern women's ego-strength. In this information age, intelligent women are breaking free of their tradition-bound past in unprecedented numbers and with unprecedented influence. This process of personal growth in independence is much easier than for their mothers and grandmothers. This is a most encouraging modern development.

A great many related influences contribute heavily to humankind's belief in the supernatural even in our scientific times. I have very briefly summarized above some of the more powerful contributors to the endurance of supernatural faith in our society. Whether it's woman power, the influence of wishful thinking, the power of hypnosis with its apparently superhuman power of prayer, the influence of longitudinal or latitudinal crowds, fear and greed for a great deal on free grace, a basic human drive to always want to progress ever further and further, or whether it is from some other source of a lack of self-confidence and self-adequacy, billions of men and women still believe in God, Allah,

Yahweh, Satan or some other Power Higher than themselves. It is important, therefore, that we examine in the next chapter the validity of that widely held premise that some power higher than thinking man exists.

SEQUITUR/NON SEQUITUR—WOMAN POWER

A man was sick and tired of going to work every day while his wife stayed home. He wanted her to see what he went through, so he prayed:

"Dear Lord, I go to work every day and put in eight hours while my wife merely stays at home. I want her to know what I go through, so please allow her body to switch with mine for a day. Amen."

God, in his infinite wisdom, granted the man's wish.

The next morning, sure enough, the man awoke as a woman. He arose, cooked breakfast for his mate, awakened the kids, set out their school clothes, fed them breakfast, packed their lunches, drove them to school, came home and packed up the dry cleaning, took it to the cleaners and stopped at the bank to make a deposit, went grocery shopping, then drove home to put away the groceries, paid the bills and balanced the checkbook. He cleaned the cat's litter box and bathed the dog. Then it was already 11:00 a.m., and he hurried to make the beds, do the laundry, vacuum, dust, and sweep and mop the kitchen floor. He ran to the school to pick up the kids and got into an argument with them on the way home. He set out cookies and milk and got the kids organized to do their homework, then set up the ironing board and watched TV while he did the ironing. At 4:30 he began peeling potatoes and washing vegetables for salad, breaded the pork chops and snapped fresh beans for supper. After supper he cleaned the kitchen, ran the dishwasher, folded laundry, bathed the kids, and put them to bed.

At 9:00 p.m. he was exhausted, and though his daily chores were not finished, he went to bed where he was expected to make love, which he managed to get through without complaint.

The next morning he awoke and immediately knelt by the bed and said, "Lord, I don't know what I was thinking. I was so wrong to envy my wife's being able to stay home all day. Please, oh please, let us trade back."

The Lord, in his infinite wisdom, replied, "My son, I feel you have learned your lesson, and I will be happy to change things back to the way they were. You'll just have to wait nine months though. You got pregnant last night."

THREE

DOES GOD EXIST?

We have already seen several psychological and historical reasons why so many believe in God or the supernatural. Now it becomes important to examine the logic that supports or undermines such faith. The first and most basic premise we must examine is whether or not there is a God, Allah, Yahweh, Satan, etc., that exists beyond nature.

BELIEVERS NEED NO PROOF

I remember well a comical encounter with a southern gentleman about 55 years old. On greeting my wife and me in a friendly fashion, he said to me, "You look familiar; did I see you in church last Sunday?" I said, "No, except for weddings and funerals, I haven't been in church in about 30 years." Well! You should have caught his reaction: "You ought to go to church to worship God and be able to go to heaven," and a few other parental type remarks that missed their mark completely. I told him that if there were a God, she must have a whale of a sense of humor. Another enthusiastic reaction as he very dogmatically stated (quoting exactly here), "God is a man!" and stalked off.

This gentleman was likely picturing God as he perceived the divinity early in life (often an artist's rendering of the human Christ). And I understand how hard it is to part with cultural ideas that were comfortably absorbed into one's experience bank in childhood. Such early impressions on the young, unquestioning mind are deep from the beginning. Add to such early impressions the repeated cultural reinforcement of such early beliefs, and you can understand how all of us tend to hold on tightly to the impressive notions from childhood. Logical proof of the veracity of such cultural mental deposits is not necessary for the majority; and logical challenge of some of those notions may even be threatening. I realize, therefore, that I may now be taking on an unpopular task.

Copernicus surely felt somewhat similarly when trying to get the flat earth society of the 1540s to see that the earth does, indeed, revolve around the sun and is not the center of the universe. The majority of Copernicus' contemporaries condemned him, but that did not change the scientific facts; the cultured majority was wrong! Likewise, the majority, accepting the traditions of popular culture, condemned Galileo, as did the same "infallible" Church authority that had condemned Copernicus; the majority was wrong again! And since the majority of humankind has been wrong repeatedly, we must not let majority opinion sway us in our examination of God's existence.

Does God exist? If he (let's grant maleness merely for ease of discussion) does exist for sure, then everyone had better do what he says! Really. But if he does not exist, then religions have no meaning beyond social organizations, and preachers, popes, and prophets have no supernatural power; so they would deserve no supernatural or superhuman respect.

Believers need no proof of God's existence. Like the Hindus

who still believe that their supreme deity, Ram, was born near Ayodhya, India, and like North American Hualapai Indians who still believe that their Grand Canyon was their Arizona Garden of Eden, believers believe authority or tradition; they don't need evidence. Reasoning humans, however, need convincing evidence in regard to such a basic and important matter as the existence of God or the supernatural.

EMOTIONAL ARGUMENTS FOR GOD'S EXISTENCE

Beauty and order in the universe argue for God's existence. It is easy to say, "Look around you, Stupid Writer. See all the wonderful beauty and precision in the universe! Where did it come from?" Yes, of course, I see a lot of beauty and order in the universe much bigger than humanity. I also see a lot of ugliness and disorder or chaos much bigger than humanity. Humankind wrestled with this problem of ugliness and evil in the world long before the biblical allegory of the Book of Job.

Can man make a sunset? Of course not; but realize the most beautiful sunsets are not mysterious or divine creations but are totally natural refractions and reflections of sunlight by the various levels of pollution and moisture in the atmosphere. The human creation of the selfless smile of a caring nurse or friend helping a cancer victim outshines the most gorgeous sunset. A sunset may be ugly for the person who desperately needs more time or daylight to find his way home; an artist at leisure may see great beauty in the very same sunset. Beauty and ugliness are created in the perception of the beholder, not by some mysterious Force beyond or above nature.

Perceived mysteries, as mysteries, argue for the supernatural. Early man looked at nature and, because of his ignorance, saw all kinds of mysterious wonders. Because of his limited understanding, he could be excused for letting his mystifying world convince him of the existence of lots of superstitions, devils, and Gods. He was surely overwhelmed by his limited knowledge of his world. Like an inexperienced child, he feared the unknowns of his mysterious world that he knew so little about, unknowns that he could neither control nor understand. So when ignorant and desperate pre-scientific man felt helpless, he prayed. In a drought he prayed to his rain-God; when hungry because the hunting was bad, he prayed to his God of the hunt; when fearful or desperate, he begged for help from the God of storms, the God of war, the God of love and more. His faith was intermittently reinforced by bountiful nature, so he believed ever more strongly in his many Gods.

When the rains came late, or the hunt was so unsuccessful that the villagers were going hungry, manipulative leaders, shamans or priests easily convinced the desperate believers to make sacrifices and give generously to appease the angry Gods. Understandably the earliest belief systems of such awe-inspired folks included an abundance of superstitions. These simple folks created lots of Gods to be respected, thanked, feared and appeased. Of course, the rains eventually came, and the hunters eventually found food; this convinced the believers that their sacrifices and offerings to the Gods and their representatives were effective.

What might have developed as our cultural heritage if ancient man, with his lack of scientific knowledge of nature, had imagined himself as a very tiny part of magnificent nature, perhaps as an ant or a little bug. The ant finds a nice crumb or bit of food dropped in its way. Does the natural ant worship or thank the unknown "litterbug" for dropping the gift from above? Or does the dung beetle worship the cow that defecates so that he has a place to roll around and have a ball? Not likely. I suspect that both the ant and the dung beetle just enjoy what came their way without any evidence of a leftover obligation to the big crapper in the sky. As far as we know, these natural animals simply appreciate nature's gifts and go on being part of nature.

Much later in human development, after appreciable philo-sophical development, by the time Marco Polo was traveling to China (1271), and by the time St. Thomas Aquinas (1225-1274) was writing his *Summa Theologica*, the majority of humankind had reached the conclusion that there must be only one God, one Highest Power in charge and that they had to worship and obey that one unknown Power.

St. Thomas Aquinas, reputedly one of the greatest philosopher-theologians of Catholic Christianity, saw the need to prove God's existence philosophically or logically. He proposed five formal proofs of God's existence, four of them being emotion based *ad hominem* arguments which I will not bother to address beyond what has already been done above. The only so-called proof that even approaches a logical proof of God's existence is "the proof from causality"; this is the one that is still seen as an effective proof by millions. This causality proof gets a bit abstract, but because it is still accepted by serious thinkers today, it must be dealt with carefully and adequately.

ST. THOMAS' CAUSALITY PROOF OF GOD

Serious minded men, looking around and seeing the great realities of nature, wonder where all this came from. St. Thomas did just that, and, since he was a respectable philosopher, he realized that everything in the world had to have an adequate cause; nothing happens by itself; nothing can cause itself. All the mutable things in this world had to be caused by something else; everything is the effect of some cause. We see Johnson (effect) and know there had to be a John (father or cause of Johnson). But John also was caused by his father and mother, so John is a secondary cause, not the primary or initial cause of Johnson. The same can be said for John's grandparents, great-grandparents, great-great-grandparents, etc. Everyone is the effect of a secondary cause. The long chain of secondary causes stretches back through history and beyond, every caused effect being a secondary cause, all the way back to an Adam, an amoeba, an atom, or whatever.

However, this chain of secondary causes cannot be infinite, said St. Thomas; it has to have a beginning; there must be a first link; it is logically, mentally abhorrent to suppose an infinite regression of secondary causes. "Therefore," concludes St. Thomas, "there must be a primary cause, a first link of that chain, and this primary cause we call God."

Now this logical "proof" convinced the Catholic Church and her theologians for centuries, the same dogmatic Church that so roundly condemned Copernicus and Galileo. It became a formal and official teaching of that church that God's existence could be rationally proven, proven purely by human reason unaided by faith. Really, this was a dogmatic teaching of the Catholic Church for centuries; it may still be.

Now if the Church were right that a good human mind un-aided by faith could actually prove God's existence, then it would behoove all of us of lesser intellects to believe in God's existence. But wait; look more closely at that "proof" that St. Thomas and his church accepted as being a proof from pure reason unaided by faith.

ST. THOMAS' GRAND ASSUMPTION EXPOSED

When St. Thomas' reason rebelled at the possibility of an infinite regression of secondary causes, an infinite chain of great-great-great-great-...-grandparents, his faith apparently took over; he simply and quite gratuitously said "therefore there must be a primary cause which we call God." This conclusion is not a conclusion of reason; it is a posited statement of faith based on ignorance: "I cannot understand my own concept of an infinite regression of secondary causes, a chain whose first link I cannot find. Therefore, rather than humbly admit that logically I have to be an agnostic, I posit, suppose, assume, believe there *must* be that first link, a primary Cause, God." Unlike Copernicus and Galileo some 200 years later, St. Thomas allowed his faith to get in the way of his science, which allowed him to draw the politically correct conclusion that God caused it all. This, in turn, allowed him to become the most respected philosopher/theologian in Christendom.

Instead of using a long chain of human secondary causes (the great-great-grandparent chain) as St. Thomas did, one could use the example of an oak table. But no matter what is used, as you approach the observable beginning, you will become an agnostic admirer of nature and humbly admit "I cannot know where the very first 'acorn' came from." Like the ant and the dung beetle that enjoyed their natural gifts from above them, I really do not need to know, so I don't need to act as though I know where it all came from. (Do you think perhaps the dung beetle considers the bull that defecates his playground to be supernatural? Surely the bull, creating this good world for the beetle, seems supernatural to the beetle. So should the balling dung beetle pay homage to such a Higher Power or just enjoy the bullshit?)

I am now embarrassed to admit that I had accepted the "logical" arguments from Saint Thomas with large crowds of other believers. I had gone through twelve years of seminary preparation, followed by post-graduate theological studies, and I still did not question adequately the validity of St. Thomas' classical "proofs" of God's existence. Just like St. Thomas, I let my faith at that time, now over forty years ago, get in the way of my reason. Back then, indeed, I enjoyed a blind and blinding faith. This embarrassing experience of mine helps me understand sympathetically the great difficulty many people have in letting go of old beliefs. We all develop at our individual rates. At the same time, I so strongly want everyone to enjoy the peace and security I have won, that I may seem impatient as I look forward to others "seeing it my way!" Many will not be able to succeed in this matter. As in the case of most victories, if success were easy, everyone would do it.

It was after about eight years in the priesthood, that I experienced that critical breakthrough and saw the inadequacy of Saint Thomas' causality "proof." I vividly recall precisely where I was in the monastery chapel doing my daily meditation on an especially insightful morning. This was really a memorable morning for me, for this was the morning I took a big personal leap from blindly credulous theism toward agnosticism.

For humankind, trying to know something beyond or above nature turns out to be an exercise in futility. It is just as impossible as the brain trying to study itself in a state of total inactivity. That effort is just as frustrating as that of the man trying to lift himself up by his own ankles or an almighty God trying to create a stone so heavy he cannot lift it. We cannot know logically or rationally about any extra-natural or supernatural being's existence. We can assume anything we choose to assume—anything—including an uncaused First Cause or a pope knowing more about reality than Galileo. Such assumptions are neither verifiable nor falsifiable. But don't forget that anything that is freely assumed can be freely denied, whether it is culturally popular or not. Any gratuitous assumption, since it is simply asserted without evidence, can be just as gratuitously denied. This principle holds both in law and in logic.

READ THE BIBLE

St. Thomas' strongest philosophical argument was based on an assumption of God; we find a similar faith-based creation of God by man in the Bible's Book of Genesis. In that book, Moses was distilling and reporting a lot of traditional stories handed down from generation to generation. At that distant time, probably about thirteen centuries before the present era (B.P.E.), he could not be expected to show the philosophical sophistication of St. Thomas some two and a half millennia later.

We can understand Moses' Book of Genesis better when we analyze very briefly how traditions develop, especially oral traditions from the hazy, pre-historic time before much writing. Families and tribes develop various beliefs, convictions, and bits of wisdom over time. These ideas are passed on as traditions within the families or tribes. When families and tribes socialize with others, they learn from each other and tell stories to impress and entertain. As they learn new things from each other, they modify their old traditions to reconcile them with more recent learnings and new insights.

This evolving process of accepting new beliefs and attempting to reconcile them with established traditions is called syncretism. Webster very simply defines syncretism as the combination of different forms of belief or practice. I like to call it the evolutionary results of faiths. The myths, stories, boasts, tales and reports from the various tribes of mankind interact on one another as they are retold from generation to generation, from tribe to tribe. The result is evolving or living tradition, that which is handed down from the past.

It will be easier to appreciate the important meaning and implications of syncretism if you put yourself in a nomadic group of desert travelers some fifteen centuries B.P.E. Your camels are staked out, supper is over, your traveling companions are all gathered around the campfire. There's no television to entertain the group, no newspaper stories to report, no books to read. Here is where the raconteur can shine as he entertains the group by sharing his stories, his experiences, real and fantasied, with his audience.

Similar sources of entertainment and news are likewise being enjoyed in other groups of travelers. And when various travelers' routes intersect at wadis or watering holes, storytelling competitions are in order for the entertainment and education of all. One tribe learns from the other, and accommodations or adaptations of knowledge bases and belief systems take place very naturally. Tribes and travelers teach each other better ways to find and preserve water, to overcome fears and feelings of inadequacy, to stay healthy and to convince the listeners that our ways are better than the ways of the strangers and competitors.

Most of us who are over fifty years old have known of modern newspaper and magazine reporters who have exaggerated and even made up stories to impress the public. For example, in the late 1990s and early 2000s, a masterfully creative liar, Stephen Glass of *The New Republic,* completely fooled his whole editorial board with his very impressive, but totally fictional "news" reports. He did it for years, because it brought him recognition for his outstanding scoops and reports. Storytellers of old were not immune from similar efforts to build their reputations.

Obviously clans tend to be clannish. So their troubadours and raconteurs easily make their heroes and accomplishments appear as great as possible. Fact and fiction readily combine to make the stories more impressive and entertaining. In this context, our heroes can beat your heroes; our superheroes are greater than yours; our Gods are better, stronger than yours. And when one person or tribe adapts old beliefs to accommodate the new, we have syncretism in action. Oral traditions are continually passed on and modified in this fashion.

Moses learned primarily from ever-changing oral tradition, since he had very little written history and no videotapes to refer to. Hearsay, therefore, was extremely important for the cultures of those ancient times.

The concept of superheroes, Gods, and religion pre-dated Moses by many centuries. Far back into prehistory, tales and myths of heroes and superheroes were part of the syncretic traditions passed from generation to generation. Such supernatural heroes and creators represent humankind's boldest attempts to give meaning to this real world. Moses wrote down the received traditions of his day and used them to his advantage.

MOSES PRESUMES GOD'S EXISTENCE

As Moses struggled hard to educate and control his people, he found a simple way to avoid admitting his ignorance of how the world turns. At least Moses, to his credit, made no pretense of proof of God; when he needed such a God, he simply posited one of the accepted syncretic stories or distilled heroic tales of tradition that God was "In the beginning…" This belief in a supernatural creator or creators of some sort was part of human tradition from time immemorial; Moses was passing along his inherited traditions.

There was a lot of chaos at that "time before time" that Moses was trying to describe in the Bible's Book of Genesis, even though he had no way of knowing about it except from those very unreliable syncretic traditions referenced above. After Moses assumed God into existence, he had God creating light before he created the sun. Vegetation and seeds of various kinds were created before the stars, and so on. Moses' report of a six-day creation of the world (and every species) surely does little to inspire confidence in anyone with even a most elementary knowledge of astronomy, geology, anthropology, biology, zoology, paleontology or any other modern science.

Yet Fundamentalists and others with limited exposure to the Bible accept that Bible as indubitable demonstration of God's existence as well as his nature and divine characteristics. These believers profess to accept every word of the Bible as inspired by an all-knowing God. It is most embarrassing for me now to realize how long I believed that the Bible was the truly inspired word of God, not word-for-word, but overall inspired and true. I showed by my own life that believers are not constrained by logic. This is why we must frequently remind ourselves to be tolerant of others who believe and develop doubts at differing individual rates.

Now, of course, I find it hard to comprehend how anyone could possibly read and understand the Bible (even half of it) and still hold its contradictions and immoralities as all being true or inspired by a wise and loving Deity. The standard response to that statement is "God works in mysterious ways." I sympathize deeply with that believing reaction, but is such a response simply another way of saying "I don't know; I am an agnostic"? It is certainly mysterious to me how I or any thoughtful person could read the Bible and overlook or discount the murders, lies, adulteries, absurd laws, and genocides that are divinely endorsed therein.

The biblical assumption of Moses regarding God as creator of everything is certainly no more and no less acceptable than St. Thomas' gratuitous assumption of God as the First Cause of everything real.

⁓

SEQUITUR/NON SEQUITUR—
SCRIPTURE PROBLEMS & FALWELL

One internet wag provided a helpful laugh at a very few of the absurd dogmatic stances based on the Bible. By way of parody, he addressed a famous American televangelist who was very big on guilt, as follows:

Dear Jerry Falwell: Thank you for doing so much to educate people regarding God's law. I have learned a great deal from your show, and try to share that knowledge with as many people as I can. When someone tries to defend the homosexual lifestyle, for example, I simply remind them that Leviticus 18:22 clearly states it to be an abomination.

I do need some advice from you, however, regarding some of the other specific laws and how to follow them:

1. When I burn a bull on the altar of sacrifice, I know it creates a pleasing odor for the Lord (Lev. 1:9). The problem is my neighbors. They claim the odor is not pleasing to them. Should I smite them?

2. I would like to sell my daughter into slavery, as sanctioned in Exodus 21:7. In this day and age, what do you think would be a fair price for her?

3. I know that I am allowed no contact with a woman while she is in her period of menstrual cleanliness (Lev. 15:19-24). The problem is, how do I tell? I have tried asking, but most women take offense.

4. Leviticus 25:44 states that I may indeed possess slaves, both male and female provided they are purchased from neighboring nations. A friend of mine claims that this applies to Mexicans but not to Canadians. Can you clarify? Why can't I own Canadians?

5. I have a neighbor who insists on working on the Sabbath. Exodus 35 clearly states he should be put to death. Am I morally obligated to kill him myself?

6. A friend of mine feels that even though eating shellfish is an abomination (Lev. 11:10) it is a lesser abomination than homosexuality. I don't agree. Can you settle this?

7. Leviticus 21:20 states that I may not approach the altar of God if I have a defect in my sight. I have to admit that I wear reading glasses. Does my vision have to be 20/20, or is there some wiggle room here?

8. Most of my male friends get their hair trimmed, including the hair around their temples, even though this is expressly forbidden by Leviticus 19:27. How should they die?

9. I know from Leviticus 11:6-8 that touching the skin of a dead pig makes me unclean, but may I still play football if I wear gloves?

10. My uncle has a farm. He violates Leviticus 19:19 by planting two different crops in the same field, as does his wife by wearing garments made of two different kinds of thread (cotton/polyester blend). He also tends to curse and blaspheme a lot. Is it really necessary that we go to all the trouble of getting the whole town together to stone them (Lev. 24:10-16)? Couldn't we just burn them to death at a private family affair like we do with people who sleep with their in-laws (Lev. 20:14)?

I know you have studied these things extensively, so I am confident you can help. Thank you again for reminding us that God's word is eternal and unchanging.

For everyone interested in enjoying a fuller appreciation of the Bible, I recommend three books: 1) *The Holy Bible;* 2) *The Born Again Skeptic's Guide to the Bible,* by Ruth Hermence Green, Freedom From Religion Foundation, 1982; and, 3) *Queen Jane's Version: The Holy Bible for Adults Only,* by Douglas A. Rankin, Dallas Emporia Press, 1995.

We have seen how emotional "proofs" of God's existence fail to convince in a scientific way. We also found that Christendom's most respected philosopher made a faith-based assumption in his best attempt to logically prove God's existence. And, since the Bible shows that the God of scriptural tradition fails miserably to measure up to modern moral standards, perhaps the best argument for atheism is the Bible itself. We must admit that, though this is certainly not a logical proof of God's non-existence, it seems to be a pretty fair pragmatic indication that the gratuitously assumed Gods of today's theologians and preachers probably do not exist. The logical positions of both the atheists and the theists are quite beyond conclusive proof, as the source of the dung beetle's heaven was beyond his comprehension. So it seems to me that philosophical agnosticism regarding either divine or hellish existences is in order. And since there is no convincing argument for letting gratuitous assumptions influence our rational human existence, the practical conclusion for me is to enjoy reasonable pursuit of happiness for myself and my planetary neighbors.

It may have been the great actress, Katherine Hepburn, who shared the following pragmatic attitude for an individual in a pluralistic society: 'Either there is a God or there is not. My believing or disbelieving does not change this fact. If there is a God and I do everything I can to lead a good life, then fine. If there is not a God and I do everything I can to lead a good life, then fine also.'

Now, let us examine whether the ideas of God and religion hurt society today.

FOUR

IS RELIGION
HARMFUL TO SOCIETY?

Charles Dickens held that "missionaries are perfect nuisances and leave every place worse than they found it." Religion, like the Bible, puts faith above reason. A necessary stance of supernatural religions is that one's faith must over-ride or control one's reason; for the believer, logic is secondary to faith. This subjecting of humankind's highest natural power to faith can lead to various sorts of illogical and destructive results: inter-faith terrorism, over-population, repression of free scientific inquiry, impoverishing the poor and ignorant contributors to dubious causes, to name a few. But I think the most destructive result of subjecting reason to faith is the loss of respect for our highest power, the logical human mind with its ability to problem solve responsibly.

Anything that undermines reliance on logical thinking and

behavior can be labeled a bunion on the foot of progress. Some of the bunions are huge; some go almost unnoticed.

MORE SOULS FOR GOD

Overpopulation is clearly one of the great causes of poverty, conflict and human misery. It is a huge bunion on the foot of progress for much of the world; and this bunion causes pain for most of the world. Nevertheless, responsible artificial birth control is officially forbidden by the powerful Catholic Church and other smaller religious bodies. In such religious circles, procreation is accompanied by God and should not be obstructed by humans. This unhampered breeding, so those believers say, enlarges the body of Christ—the more souls for God, the better.

Should the pope be challenged or held responsible when a poor, believing mother of five in south Texas says to their overburdened father: "I just don't know how we can afford another child; I trust God will provide! God will give us another bundle of joy from heaven with an immortal soul." Credulous parents cooperate with God, create more souls, so they do more of God's will? It seems to be the will of the pope anyhow. Would that the pope pick up some of the extra tax burdens based on over-population and the resultant ignorance, disease and poverty!

A soul created in God's image, religionists hold, is of infinite value even if that new life (well-formed or mal-formed) resulted from ignorance, rape, incest or immature carelessness. Often missionaries preaching their gospel refuse to teach birth control or the responsible handling of human fertility even in the poorest and already overpopulated areas. Then those same missionaries send pathetic pictures of the starving and diseased children back home to tug at the heart strings of caring human beings in their cunning attempts to raise funds to support more missionary work. Irresponsible over-breeding shown in the large numbers of sick and starving street urchins expanding "the body of Christ" throughout the world is a glaring example of how religion hurts society far more than is generally recognized.

Actually the Catholic Church does want more and more people on earth. Every person is of infinite or immortal value. It makes little difference, it seems, that those multiplying members live in demeaning poverty and squalor as they overtax the infrastructure of, for example, Mexico City. Those twenty million or so Catholics, where there ought to be perhaps less than half that many residents, are still counted as Catholics. They help make the membership numbers look good. They buy religious jewelry and votive candles, put money in offertory baskets and alms boxes; and, perhaps more important, those large membership numbers increase ecclesiastical power. These large masses believe that popes, cardinals, bishops, and priests (all male, incidentally) represent God. This faith provides abundant cheap power and political influence.

CHEAP DIVINE POWER

Such divinity-based power has influenced the history of the world. It worked for Moses; it worked for kings with so-called divine rights (*gratia Dei Rex*). It continues to work today for ministers, priests, bishops, popes, rabbis and mullahs of all stripes. "By the grace of God, I claim to represent him (and a lot of votes!), so you'd better follow me and my divinely inspired controls. I have divine authority to tell you how to pursue happiness."

Catholic and Protestant seminaries get control of naïve and brainwashed youngsters and send them forth to convert the world. So Jehovah's enthusiastic witnesses come in many flavors and represent thousands of faith systems reaching to the ends of the earth for God, Christ, Allah, Yahweh or Jehovah. These missionaries must first become humble, lowly little children before they can become naïve and credulous enough to do their superiors' sales work, sometimes in life-threatening circumstances, with little or no commission. Such missionaries can be deeply offensive to freedom-loving, informed twenty-first century adults. Overt preaching of their divine mysteries is offensive enough, but the offense can be worse when the messages are surreptitiously snuck in with the beats of the rocker or the cadences of the rapper.

SERVICE TO THE NEEDY OR
POWER AND INFLUENCE

A little noticed but very noteworthy bit of news was reported by CNN TV on February 12, 2002. It showed again the competitive divisiveness of religions. "Roman Catholic Church establishes diocesan organization for Russia; Orthodox Church strenuously objects." What goes on here? The Roman Church and Orthodox Church claim the same God. Their belief systems and dogmas are almost identical. So why wouldn't each one welcome the other to help teach the truth and do the many undone acts of Christian charity?

On the very next day, the Associated Press reported that the head of the Roman Catholic Church in Russia strongly denied that the Vatican's decision to set up four dioceses in the country was aimed at expanding its influence in this predominantly Orthodox Christian nation. How obvious does a lie have to be before meriting that label?

The central problem here is not what is truth and who should teach it; the real problem is sales turf and power. Dare the Russian Orthodox Church allow such a big and strong organization as the Roman Catholic diocesan set-up to come into Russia? The fear is of competition for souls (loyalties) and sales—influence and profits. "We have our turf, and we don't want you Roman Catholics to invade this turf." The Russian Holy Synod did not actually suspend contacts with the Vatican, but the Russian officials had threatened to do so, saying that proselytizing was a major obstacle to better relations. So here is the big news: in line with Dickens' thought, proselytizing is divisive.

This Russian-Roman situation seems like one large company competing with another. These two big competitors are both selling the same products by the same methods. But if they share the same turf, they might have to divide the influence and income.

Therein lies the rub. Loyalties and devotees might be divided thus diminishing someone's power, influence, and income.

MULTITUDES OF RELIGIONS, MULTITUDES OF DIVISIONS

This divisive competition between the Roman Catholic and Russian Orthodox Churches is not very different from that between the thousands of religions here in America. *Time's Almanac 2000* reported at least 29 so-called Christian religions that claim at least 500,000 members each. Besides these 29 sizeable groups, there are over 3,000 smaller "Christian" groups, who, even though they cannot get along together nor agree on what is true, claim to instruct and unify good human beings.

The above refers only to the many Christian divisions in our society. Non-Christian religions expand the divisions of our citizenry even further. I doubt that my prayer inscribed on my new gold chalice in 1956 "that we all may be one" is going to be answered for a long while.

It's in the book. Holy books dogmatically divide humanity with divinely inspired authority: the Bible tells me this; the Koran tells others that; the Book of Mormon tells of yet other revelations of divine truth; the Vedas reveal the truths of Hinduism; Buddhism enlightens us further about the Tree of Perfect Knowledge as early as the fifth century before the present era; and Taoism showed humankind the True Way at about the same time.

The similarities, differences, and contradictions within and among the major religious groupings accepting these various revelations demonstrate the infinity of the human imagination. They also show that once a dogma of a supernatural faith system is assumed to be true, then logic and human reason become secondary or unimportant. And once reason is de-based and not considered man's highest power, any extreme of faith can be reached: popes become infallible; virgin births become possible; logical contradictions do not pertain to the Holy Trinity; and, dying defending your faith against another defending his faith against you is eternally meritorious.

Martyrdom, by the way, did not start with middle eastern Muslims. The eternal value of martyrdom was a manipulative tenet of the Christian Church from earliest days. The Church officially taught from antiquity that anyone who dies actively defending the Church and its faith dies a martyr's death and goes directly to heaven. Do all these varied warring martyrs finally find unified bliss in their heaven? Which heaven? Perhaps the Roman heaven with Jupiter and Juno (Mrs. Jupiter)? Or perhaps the Greek heaven of Zeus and Hera (Mrs. Zeus)?

The god concept, since it is not evidence-based but is based on subjective and logic-free faith, necessarily remains different things for different people. I think it will remain so until we quit assuming that there is any power higher than man's logical and unifying reason. In America, cults are broadly condemned, while religions are generally approved. I find it extremely difficult to distinguish between a religion and a cult. In fact, the more experienced I become, the harder it becomes for me to distinguish between cult and religion. Webster's Dictionary certainly does not help in this important matter.

Is a religion just a more popular cult? What is the real and basic difference anyway? Is it purely a matter of personal opinion or belief? Is it a matter of numbers? Is it perhaps dependent on how long the group has stayed together? Is the Branch Davidians more a religion than a cult, or vice versa? Ask the same question of yourself regarding, say, Mormons, Seventh Day Adventists, Moonies, Pentecostals, Catholics, Lutherans, Baptists (which sections?), etc., any of those heretical groups other than the one you might believe in. Here we find further foundation for the multiplicity of divisions of citizens. It seems much harder to unite "under God" than "under reason."

RELIGION CAN CONTRIBUTE TO MENTAL LAZINESS
St. Paul wrote that faith is the foundation of things hoped for,

the explanation of things unseen. And the poet Robert Browning wrote "Ah, that man's reach exceeds his grasp, or what's a heaven for?" This basic and commonly felt desire for more than man can actually achieve creates a wish-fulfilling heaven for many. On the other hand, it energizes curious, rational, scientific minds ever further in their pursuit of knowledge of the real facts of life. The former see a lot of supernatural mysteries and miracles with God solving human problems; the latter work hard building better microscopes, spectroscopes, and computers to expand human knowledge and dissolve the mysteries of ignorance.

Recall that the original sin against God in Moses' Garden of Eden, as described in his biblical story in the Book of Genesis, was man's desire for knowledge. Adam and Eve (more correctly, "Man and Woman" or "Male and Female") were given totally free access to all the delights of the Garden of Eden with one very important exception: they were not allowed to eat of the Tree of Knowledge. Well, you probably know the rest of the story, how Satan (Snake) tempted Eve, Eve tempted Adam, and they both ate of "the Tree of Knowledge." Having eaten of this specially forbidden tree, having committed The Original Sin, they discovered they were naked, became ashamed of their good bodies, and were kicked out of the beautiful Garden of Eden.

And what was God's specific punishment for Adam and Eve and all their descendants for this curious seeking of knowledge? "In the sweat of your brow shall you eat bread." Ah, ha; now man has to work in order to eat. What a shame! And the very natural and reasonable tenet that man has to work in order to eat is a hard reality for the lazy. It is surely not nearly as hard as the reality for the little fish swimming his tail off trying not to get eaten by the big fish. Did you ever wonder what that little fish's original sin was? Why does he have to work so hard to stay alive or else suffer and die so that the big fish might live?

It is so much easier for some to "believe and be saved" from such harsh natural reality—all things are possible for him who believes; the Bible tells me so. Therefore, just believe and you'll be saved; ask the ignorant poor in a soup line waiting for a free handout. Their faith assures them that God will provide! But some sweaty human being first has to kill an innocent turkey.

The oldest Catholic order of monks, the Benedictines, have a central tenet: *Ora et labora*, pray and work. When I belonged to that order of monks, yet another of the thousands of divisions within the Christian Churches, we were taught to pray as if all depended on God, but work as if all depended on us. Is that a can't-lose or a can't-win arrangement?

HISTORIC GOD, THE GOD OF WARS AND DIVISIONS

The horribly destructive and divisive power of an assumed powerful God of war is all too evident from ancient history to modern times. The following is a very brief summary of glaring examples of this phenomenon.

Much of the Bible details the merciless fighting, killing, raping and pillaging in God's name. "He smites mine enemies" over and over and over. Joshua, if the Bible is reliable, had God's help in taking lands from their just owners. He even had the sun and moon (time) stand still so he could take full revenge on his enemies before darkness set in. See, it really helps to have God on your side. The Old testament's King Saul and the most famous King David recognized this repeatedly. (However, it was surely not completely according to God's plan that David would send Uriah, Bathsheba's husband, to get killed in battle as David hung back so that he could get together romantically with Bathsheba.)

Constantine the Great, who legalized Christianity by the Edict of Milan in 313, fought hard and effectively in the name of God. He re-united the Eastern and Western Roman Empire using sword and cross. Finally this great warlord formally and belatedly became a Christian on his deathbed in 337. (Was he just covering his rear in fear?) Forty-three years later, Emperor Theodosius proclaimed Christianity to be the state religion; other religions were suppressed. Within half a century the Roman empire had disintegrated.

For its part, the Muslim empire grew from nothing right after 600 to become strong enough that its religious fighters could conquer Jerusalem by 637. By this time, the Muslim calendar was only fifteen years old. Four years later these religious enthusiasts "succeeded" in destroying that greatest world center of culture and wisdom, the great library at Alexandria (641). Less than 100 years after Mohammed fled from Mecca to Medina, these warriors for Allah had extended their Arabian Empire from Spain to China. This devotion to a Higher Power obviously drives believing devotees to extreme achievement. (Allah beats God?) How much further ahead would real and positive human wisdom be if the library of Alexandria had not been lost to humankind! Again religion gets in the way of human wisdom and progress.

The unhealthy union of Church and State or Cross and Crown was cemented in the West in 800 when Charlemagne was crowned the First Holy Roman Emperor. The Muslims had already shown how successfully they could unite sword and crescent in the East.

Muslim warriors destroyed the Holy Sepulcher in Jerusalem in 1009. The Church did not like this. When much later (1096) Pope Urban II started the First Crusade, it was billed primarily as a holy war to take control of Jerusalem from the Muslims. The Warrior Pope promised all kinds of indulgences and spiritual rewards to his Crusaders for Christ. If a soldier died as a martyr fighting the infidels (Muslims), he was rewarded with heaven! Sound familiar? Thus, in cooperation with Emperor Alexius I, the faith-based initiative called the First Crusade, captured Jerusalem for the Christians in 1099. This was a great Christian victory. (God beat Allah this time?)

Toward the end of the twelfth century, another Holy War, this time a Muslim *jihad*, united Islam so strongly that they could retake Jerusalem (1187). This faith-based war took place after the abject failure of the Second Crusade under the Holy Roman Emperor Conrad III and Catholic King Louis VIII of France in

1147. (Allah beats God this time?) In fact, the Christian side also lost Crusades IV to VIII (1200—1270).

Probably the most disgraceful of all the many Christian religious Crusades was the so-called Children's Crusade. In 1212 some 50,000 French and German children marched east to fight for Christ's cause. Only about a miserable 200 returned. The others likely had believed they would be enjoying heaven. How different was this religion-based abuse of the credulous and immature from what we saw with the brainwashed suicide bombers of the Middle East?

When a credulous human being is incapable of independent thinking, he can be led to almost any irrational belief and extreme pursuit. When one becomes a believer in the naturally impossible, reason's discriminating power diminishes, and the spiritual leader can have near total control. When the leader becomes fanatical or divinely enthusiastic, he demonstrates again the old adage: power corrupts, and absolute power corrupts absolutely.

The modern fight in the Middle East between the descendents of the biblical sons of Abraham has been going on for too many centuries. It is likely to go on for more centuries unless these fervent believers in their divisive religious traditions can break free to think rationally and eat of the Tree of Knowledge or science. This demands an abundance of rational educational efforts.

Osama bin Laden, by his terrorist fighting, according to many, has shown himself to be a true Muslim, fighting the *jihad* as commanded by Mohammed as Allah's prophet in accord with the Koran. I am confident that moderate Muslims are offended by bin Laden's extreme position, but such is the blinding power of faith in God once reason is overcome by that faith.

In the Bible's Old Testament reports of the battles of God's chosen people, you find repeated reports of worse religious attacks on the heathens and infidels than bin Laden was guilty of. Moses, Joshua, David and many less famous fighters of the Old Testament were as bloody as bin Laden and modern believers in Mohammed fighting their own *jihads* in the name of Allah. Justifications of holy wars are abundantly plain in the scriptural revelations from both Allah and Yahweh. And that other middle eastern religious founder, Jesus, reputedly said he came not to bring peace, but the sword. Pick a war-torn period, pick a war or ethnic division, and you are very likely to find it has deeply religious roots.

Have the ravages of divine violence and faith-based initiatives gone on long enough to drive honest, thinking men to the negotiating tables? How long must humankind repeat that he who does not learn the lessons of history is condemned to repeat them? Who do you think ought to go first in admitting the destructiveness of holy wars: Algeria, Bosnia, Chechnya, Egypt, India, Indonesia, Iran, Ireland, Iraq, Israel, Kashmir, Kosovo, Lebanon, Nigeria, Pakistan, Palestine, Philippines, Somalia, Sudan, Turkey, U.K., U.S.A. or who?

ENEMIES OF GOD MUST BE DESTROYED

Why do religionists think their almighty God needs help in smiting his enemies? Old Testament Jews did it, and created enemies of long standing. Early Christians did it, and modern Christians still do it. Seventh Century Muslims did it, and modern Muslims still do it. George W. Bush got a God-like strength and enthusiastic political backing for the bombing attacks on al Qaeda terror groups in Afghanistan in 2001 and 2002. Such use of righteous power to smite the axis of evil still makes enemies around the world. These enemies made in the name of righteousness readily remind one of the many enmities the warring Chosen People made on their way from Egypt to the Promised Land in and around Jerusalem.

TRADITION, TRADITION, COSTLY, RETROGRESSIVE TRADITION

Why is it so important that one religious group triumph over another? Is it tradition and the intransigent need to enshrine the "sacred" past? Nature put eyes in the front of our heads so we can look forward. However, today's bellicose believers seem so hung up on the dark ages of ancient beliefs and the hand-me-downs of syncretism that they cannot let go of prejudices against progress. Buried places of worship in old Palestine, wailing walls, especially sacred shrines, and so-called promised lands take on non-negotiable value because of traditional beliefs, beliefs based on ancient, megalomanic false assumptions that have long outlasted their real value.

The fratricidal fight between Jews and Palestinians will likely go on for more centuries unless these fervent believers in their religious traditions can become free enough to analyze their holy traditions and think rationally about the present. Bertrand Russell held correctly that the first requirement for becoming a freethinker is to get free from the force of tradition. This freedom demands that thoughtful efforts replace blind faith in "sacred" traditions that justify bullying by bombs and bullets. We Are Righteous! We Are Right!

I have a lot of hope for the human race, but I don't see much reason to think that the Mid-East problem involving the so-called holy places will ever see peace in this generation. "There will always be wars and rumors of war" is one prophecy attributed to Christ that remains true of the biblical Middle East.

Sarajevo and Serbia, Israel and Ireland, along with too many other countries, can cry over lost prosperity and what might have been without religious/ethnic wars. Religion causes war causes poverty causes human desperation causes religion, causes war, causes poverty—and the beat goes on and on. This vicious cycle demands tremendous effort to break. The Mid-East, cradle of three competitive, traditionally Abrahamic religions, Judaism, Christianity and Islam, remains so deeply mired in old hates and traditions that stable peace and prosperity still seem impossible. Again, as Christ predicted, they will always have the poor with them.

I wonder, though, what would happen if the believers in Yahweh, Allah, and Christ were to decide to assume for just a day that God does not really exist, that these outdated buildings and places are not really holy, that you (other) "bad" guys resemble us "good" guys, that we are really quite like each other. You guys get hungry, tired, lonely, rejoice, make love just like we do. Can we think together, negotiate about real, measurable things, leave out our superstitions, the mysterious and immeasurable, while we make practical, rational deals?

See, the sky doesn't fall when we set aside, even for a day, such an outmoded and outrageous assumption based on superstition. What is freely or groundlessly asserted, can be freely denied. We can now see each other more clearly, now that we are not blinded and looking backward because of a blind or unreasoning faith. We can see much more of current reality now that we no longer obsess about the mysterious, out-of-this-world past. Let's enjoy together now what we know we share in nature.

In the Dark Ages of the Christian Faith, almost everyone assumed the earth was flat; the sky didn't fall when almost everyone quit believing that; the sky didn't fall when Christian beliefs did away with Jupiter and Zeus. And the sky certainly didn't fall in the last decade as the portion of American non-believers increased from about eight percent to about 14% of the population. Don't be afraid to think! Don't be afraid to eat of the tree of new knowledge!

"Oh, sure, Skeptical Writer, you can abuse your freedom and deny God now, but you will suffer terribly for it; you will go to hell and suffer forever," say many of the conventionally credulous. Well, for many years I myself really believed that. But now I don't think hell is feasible; so I deny your assumption. I can now see that your improbable statement is based on counterproductive tradition. And that outmoded tradition can be traced to the gratuitous manipulative assumption found in the Book of Genesis.

When I die before long, I will make room for Nature to handle another world citizen. And whether or not that new citizen is wiser than you or me in deciding which traditions to accept and which to reject, it won't make any difference at all to me after I'm dead. I will have completed a full life, as full as it will ever get. I have overcome that most common defense, wishful thinking. I don't expect or wish for more than the great opportunities, loves, and riches that this current life has afforded me in wonderful abundance.

MORE NON-PRODUCTIVE CUSTOMS AND TRADITIONS

A story is told of the young housewife who always cut the shank portion off the Christmas ham before baking it along with the main part of the ham. Her husband asked her why she always did that; he didn't see any reason for that extra step. His wife said, "I don't know. Mom always did it that way." So later on Christmas Day, the husband asked his mother-in-law, "Mom, why did you always cut the shank off the ham before baking it; your daughter couldn't tell me why she does it." Mom: "Well, I always had to cut off the shank because my baking pan was too short."

So very many customs made sense in the past but have outlived their utility. With much better access to facts today, we are leaping ahead of the recent past; we are becoming far more productive of real goods and services than any generation in the past. It used to make sense to take days to communicate personal thoughts and messages by snail-mail; now we commonly use e-mail, faxes, and phones. It used to make sense to put some oats and water in the vehicle before beginning a long journey. Now we have better ways; we get quicker and greater horsepower without the oats.

In less developed segments of society, a lot of time is spent on pageantry, processions and liturgical ceremonies glorifying the past; more progressive societies spend less and less time commemorating the past, and this leaves more time to spend enjoying present realities and learning of future possibilities. Such freedom from the past allows a freer, more creatively productive approach to the future.

The very best use of the wisdom of the past is as a teacher. History should show us, not just what was good and productive, but also how we can grow beyond the customs and practices of the past to become more perceptive of current realities. A good teacher shines the light of history onto the realities of the present in order to see more in the future. A God teacher uses history to preserve ancient faith systems, keeping the "sacred" past, enshrining old ways and customs as though they already contained all wisdom.

Credulous devotees who place their faith in the preachments of rabbis, priests, preachers, mullahs, bishops and popes do not develop the ego-strength and independent thought to ask why: Why do we continue to cut the shank off the ham? Why do we continue to spend so much time wandering in the desert of past mysteries? Why do we continue to weep and wail at a wall that preserves old hates and blocks vision to the future? Why do we continue to run around in liturgical circles letting these religious leaders continue to tell us we are guilty of crimes of many generations ago? Why should we twenty-first century thinkers sheepishly imitate our forefathers in unthinking faith when we can realistically admit we can learn more about present realities and future probabilities than our ancestors ever could? Why do we kill each other to claim the so-called holy land where hatreds and religious divisions strive to justify such old insanities? Is it because science/ knowledge is hard to come by?

Knowledge and practical wisdom have to be worked for; the easy, superstitious, logic-free assumptions of faith don't cut it in the twenty-first century. Get over the past, Jew, Gentile, Christian, Muslim, Hindu. Tear up your sacred martyrdom manuals; back away from your traditional wailing walls; wake up and smile at the wonderful present. Try, just one day at a time, to be courageous enough, reasonable enough to ask why—why should I believe manipulators who want to use me for their empire? Why should I hate anyone who believes or thinks differently than I? I am free, and I can patiently show my less fortunate neighbors how much joy that freedom to think for myself can bring.

MODERN YOUNG MINDS POLLUTED BY RELIGION

A good teacher instills curiosity about facts in his students; a religion teacher too often demands rote memorization of manipulative catch phrases and passages from the Bible, Koran, Talmud, Book of Mormon, catechism, old revelations, traditions and worn out assumptions. The good teacher motivates students to ask why and why not; the God teacher demands unquestioning faith in what used to be believed by the faithful in darker ages. The one helps the next generation to spiral upwards to new knowledge; the other helps the next generation to repeat the mistakes of old. The one shows the way to human advancement; the other claims to already be the way, the truth and the life. So the one increases human knowledge and self-reliance, while the other continues the endless wandering in the desert of ignorant credulity and manipulable lack of confidence in self.

Today, as in the past, religion often holds kids back, brainwashes and deceives them. As recently as October 2002, Pope John Paul II told Catholic kids to babble an expanded and "improved" version of the fifty-times-repetitive Rosary. It only takes about twenty minutes a day. Can you imagine any thinking person repeating the same prayer fifty times in twenty minutes? Please! It would be so much more productive to have these busy and naturally curious youngsters studying realities of math and science than babbling hypnogenic, repetitive, brainwashing messages of myths and mysteries. The brighter ones among the curious youngsters may well ask if this papal recommendation showed the aging pontiff's senility more than divine inspiration.

Pope John Paul II's Apostolic letter *Rosarium Virginis Mariae (Rosary of the Virgin Mary)* proclaimed to all the world that October 2002 to October 2003 was the Year of the Rosary. He wrote: "The Rosary ... offers a familiar yet fruitful spiritual and educational opportunity for ... the new evangelization." Later in the same letter, he wrote: "To pray the Rosary is to hand over our burdens to the merciful hearts of Christ and his mother."

The Rosary, with its hypnogenic repetitions has probably done more to bring Catholics to their knees both physically and mentally than perhaps any other religious practice after baptism. The following section is for those of you not familiar with the details of how millions of Catholics have said the Rosary for many decades.

HOW TO PRAY THE ROSARY

1. While holding the crucifix make the Sign of the Cross, and then recite the "Apostles' Creed" (text below).
2. Recite the "Our Father" holding the first large bead.
3. On each of the three small beads recite a "Hail Mary" (text below) for an increase of faith, hope, and charity.
4. Recite the "Glory be to the Father" (text below) on the next large bead.
5. Recite the "Our Father" on the next large bead.
6. On each of the adjacent ten small beads (also referred to as a decade) recite a "Hail Mary."
7. On the next large bead, recite the "Glory Be to the Father."
8. Each of five decades is prayed in a similar manner by reciting the "Our Father," ten "Hail Marys", and the "Glory Be to the Father."
9. When the fifth decade is completed, the Rosary is customarily concluded with the "Hail, Holy Queen."

* * *

APOSTLES' CREED—

I BELIEVE in God, the Father Almighty, Creator of heaven and earth; and in Jesus Christ, his only Son, our Lord, who was conceived by the Holy Ghost, born of the Virgin Mary, suffered under Pontius Pilate, was crucified, died and was buried. He descended into hell; the third day he arose again from the dead. He ascended into heaven, sitteth at the right hand of God the Father

Almighty; from thence he shall come to judge the living and the dead. I believe in the Holy Ghost, the Holy Catholic Church, the Communion of Saints, the forgiveness of sins, the resurrection of the body, and life everlasting. Amen.

* * *

HAIL MARY—

HAIL MARY, full of grace; the Lord is with thee; blessed art thou among women, and blessed is the fruit of thy womb, Jesus. Holy Mary, Mother of God, pray for us sinners, now and at the hour of our death. Amen.

* * *

OUR FATHER—

OUR FATHER, who art in heaven, hallowed be thy name; thy kingdom come; thy will be done on earth as it is in heaven. Give us this day our daily bread, and forgive us our trespasses as we forgive those who trespass against us. And lead us not into temptation, but deliver us from evil. Amen.

* * *

GLORY BE—

GLORY BE to the Father, and to the Son, and to the Holy Ghost; as it was in the beginning, is now, and ever shall be, world without end. Amen.

* * *

HAIL HOLY QUEEN—

HAIL, HOLY QUEEN, Mother of Mercy! our life, our sweetness, and our hope! To thee do we cry, poor banished children of Eve; to thee do we send up our sighs, mourning and weeping in this valley of tears. Turn, then, most gracious Advocate, thine eyes of mercy toward us; and after this our exile, show unto us the blessed fruit of thy womb, Jesus. Oh clement, Oh loving, Oh sweet Virgin Mary. Pray for us, Oh Holy Mother of God, that we may be made worthy of the promises of Christ.

The above section tells you how you can pray the Rosary. If you want the Catholic Church's detailed instructions as to how to perform exorcisms or cast out devils, you can find the directions in the 84 page *Roman Ritual*. This ritual was recently revised, so I am not making up the fact that the Church of Rome still believes in the existence of the Devil and that he can take possession of some human beings. There was quite an upsurge in calls for exorcisms after the popular film, *The Exorcist*, was so successful in theaters, another example of the influence of the crowd on individual belief systems.

It took me a long time to appreciate how my old conventional religion promoted my wandering in the desert of credulity. The following illustrates how modern religion continues, in a more subtle way, to prolong old beliefs. In early 2002 some local youths were helping in neighborhood clean-ups while being treated to music and rap sessions along with the pop theology of the friendly Reverend Mr. Hill. After some of the youngsters' questions of their reverend leader, it became clear that these impressionable young people had learned that "there are no toilets in heaven, but, yes, there are dogs (any fire-hydrants?) in heaven, and God has a beard, maybe, maybe not!" (Rev. Hill wasn't sure of this one!) I now recall that when I was a kid in grade school we asked the nun the same question about dogs in heaven. She said, somewhat more correctly than Rev. Mr. hill, "If you want a dog in heaven, you will have your dog in heaven." This dear, lovable nun, Sister Mary Phillip, was safe in saying that *if*, after we died, we still wanted a dog, we could have it.

I do not want to argue with the Rev. Mr. hill about toilets, dogs, beards, or other anthropomorphisms in heaven. I now prefer to question the unquestioned implication that there is a heaven at all—though these children would not ordinarily think to question that more basic assumption. I wish mentors of such youngsters could help them become generous and environmentally sensitive without implying the improbable for their open young minds.

Yet another example of the counter-productivity of religious teaching is the use of the fear of hell to keep Christians in line. When I was a child, our parish was Saint Michael's. I remember vividly a very colorful statue of Saint Michael the archangel (as a handsome young man with wings) spearing the snake over a pit showing suffering souls in horrible flames. This statue of quite dubious taste had a prominent and impressive position in the sanctuary as long as I can remember. It helped make any sermons on the pains of hell quite impressive to me in my grade school days.

As a naïve youngster I was no mental match for a big person with glorifying robes who spoke from on high with an authority representing God. Such a bigger-than-human-life figure deeply influenced me, and surely impeded my natural drive toward rationality. You can likely relate to similar early influences in your own youth. From your own personal experience, you can probably relate to the difficulty of overcoming these logic-free messages from those who were then accepted as fully trustworthy messengers of truth. All of us believed before we were able to think. That's one of the reasons it is so difficult to let reason reign supreme when emotions conflict with it. Be patient with self and tolerant of others while you keep trying to think ever more clearly.

I succeeded in healing my scars only after years of challenging battles and extensive study. I heartily encourage you not to shy away from the necessary fight for the mental freedom of logical consistency—of being true to your highest power, your logical intellect. What an exhilarating freedom! It is worth battling for.

During my personal battle for mental freedom, I was more fortunate than most. In 1965, I had a near-fatal auto crash. Being late for an appointment, I was in a hurry as I topped a hill on a familiar country road near Marmion. Since there was a steep drop-off to the right, it seemed impossible to avoid a high-speed, head-on collision with a car coming up the middle of the road. Recall that at that time I was still a priest, though I was in the midst of my multi-year intellectual or spiritual struggle.

When I saw that car coming at me in my right-of-way, I was completely convinced that I was a dead man. I locked up the brakes, and yes, I prayed. But it was truly an agnostic's prayer that went something like this: "God, help me; have mercy on my soul if I need it—if you are there!" Then I lost consciousness.

When I was waking up from that painless and peaceful state, I repeatedly experienced varied lights that many unscientific writers about near-death experiences have called supernatural. Several who heard the crash and saw the car thought it was a miracle I survived; it wasn't. I can explain it all naturally. Before the accident, I was in good physical shape and thirty-five years young. So I was able to stay in the car instead of crashing through the windshield. After the accident, I was fortunate enough to be near some very scientific and talented trauma specialists. They did a great job on my body! However, that wasn't the best part of the good break I got from this terrible accident.

The best thing to come from this accident for me was the deepest recognition that I was really a sincere agnostic and that I was not a victim of the self-deception of wish fulfillment when I considered myself an agnostic. Realize that this incident happened after I had already been debating my theological position within myself for well over a year. In that "moment of truth" when I was staring death squarely in the face, my prayer for God's help and mercy was conditional: "...*if* you are there, *if* you exist." At that time I became certain that I honestly doubted whether or not there was any God. Consequently, finalizing my difficult decision to leave the priesthood and the Catholic Church immediately became far easier for me. I now had to do it to avoid hypocrisy, to be true to myself.

I can sympathize deeply with any conscientious reader fighting to get free from childhood biases and prejudices. It is hard to get free from the engrained past. Family and ethnic customs are instilled before reason reigns. I hope such a book as this will help you be true to yourself without the need of such a serious accident as I had.

My development from agnosticism to atheism took place gradually and naturally over the next several years. As a philosophical agnostic who no longer had a blinding faith in God, it was easier for me to see the practical implications from "evil." By "evil" I do not mean "sin" or "being bad" as moralists consider evil. Such things as prejudicial hatred, self-induced cancer from smoking, disastrous car crashes, poverty based on laziness, and heart disease based on personal neglect; these are not sins or evil; they are examples of irresponsibility or abuse of personal freedom.

Here I am referring to the "evil" of nature that man has no control of. Hurricanes, earthquakes, tornadoes, floods, and droughts with their disastrous effects on innocent and powerless sufferers. These remind me of the disaster that happens to the ant when a person or animal walks on it and thoughtlessly crushes it. These powerful happenings are nature in the raw, as are the squeals of a rabbit caught in the hungry jaws of a predator fox.

Seeing this sort of evil in nature, I gradually came to the conclusion that there could be no loving, caring, almighty God, either as author or guide of such a system of suffering. If a God saw such evil or created or permitted it, he would be more sadistic than loving. What remains is nature, with all its power, brutality, and beauty—nature, this huge self-contained eco-system of universes into which all of us must fit.

Now it is a lot easier to follow where reason leads me, to responsibly follow my highest power without blinding prejudices and juvenile credulity. The personal peace that results from such a heightened ability to be true to my rational self is so good for me that I want it to be shared by everyone. You will see, if you observe nature closely, that even in the painful predator-prey world, those species that cooperate survive longer and live better than if they did not cooperate. It somehow does not seem natural for members of *species homo sapiens* to prey on one another.

This is precisely why I write this book. My hope and my goal is for lasting peace firmly based on the rational Golden Rule, which says: treat others as you would reasonably want and expect them to treat you if your roles were reversed. This is a fond hope, a very tall order, I know. But it can happen, because the predator-prey relationship within a species seems unnatural and illogical. (We will see later how the consistent observance of The Golden Rule shows truly *enlightened selfishness*; it pays handsome dividends.)

CREDULITY CAN IMPEDE CREATIVE RESEARCH

Yet another example of how religious dogma can get in the way of progress showed itself on April 10, 2002. George W. Bush proclaimed very dogmatically on national television that human life is a divine creation, not a commodity. Therefore, according to his dogmatic opinion, human cloning must never take place. The president's statement oversimplifies and presents a false dichotomy, which implies that all human life is either a divine creation or a commodity. Believers who abhor therapeutic cloning claim dogmatically that two or four cells of a zygote constitute a human being. I think a human being is far more complex and can hardly be smaller than a pin head. In any event, real human life is ours to improve cooperatively. Hopefully the U.S. Congress will show more scientific knowledge than this conservative right-wing president and allow research in this important area to advance. If not, the United States may quickly fall behind the scientists in other countries, for holding onto the past too conservatively or too dogmatically will again impede progress into the future. Futurist

Peter Schwartz predicts that as "the U.S. continues to debate the morality of cloning, China will take up the slack. It already has begun state-funded stem-cell research." (Forbes Magazine, July 21, 2003, p. 50)

Creative and intelligent researchers want to use cloning as they try to win the tough battles against Parkinson's Disease, diabetes, Alzheimer's Disease and other ills. If they are to fight these tough battles in U.S. laboratories, they may be forced to do so with questioned legality or work with one hand tied behind their backs. I hope the courage of these creative scientists will be great enough to overcome the obstructive pressures of narrow dogmatism, even if such dogmatism reflects current majority opinion.

The majority's opinion deserves respect in matters purely political; however, popular opinion should get little respect in scientific matters, because scientists look for facts, not votes. Galileo, Copernicus and Newton were in very small minorities! Galileo was imprisoned by the Catholic Inquisition, because he insisted that the earth was not really the center of the universe. This imprisonment of a heretical scientist by traditional authority looks truly ridiculous now, but it didn't seem so in 1634. Popular thinking has changed a lot since then; it can continue to improve as our education continues to improve and frees us further from old dogma.

I think we can learn enough from historic mistakes to help the next generation avoid a lot of them. We as individuals, parents and politicians can become educated and self-sufficient enough, have enough pride and self-respect to drop divisive superstitions from our lives. If each of us does so, then we will experience a brand new birth of freedom that will never again be lost to blinding forces that some consider above nature. This new birth will likely be easier for the young adults than for the grayer generations. In his commencement speech at Stanford University in 2005, Steve Jobs, founder of Apple Computer, gave the graduates some excellent advice: "Your time is limited, so don't waste it living someone else's life. Don't be trapped by dogma which is living with the results of other people's thinking. Don't let the noise of others' opinions drown out your own inner voice."

If no one were to read the horoscope, newspapers would quit publishing it. If no one of us ever lied to a legitimately credulous child again, that absorbent mind would be more likely to respect reason, study math and science early in life, and help find cures for some of humankind's real problems. If no one supposed anything greater than nature, our young and bright would be freer to understand much more of nature than our own past-oriented, tradition-bound generation.

Such persons, being freer from the past, would generally be much more open to the present than the following very nice neighbor lady demonstrated: recently we were enjoying a fine dinner together with other friends when the subject of evolution came up, very briefly as it turned out. As soon as the subject was mentioned, this charming lady flatly stated, "I don't accept evolution; I believe in the bible." And with that the subject was dropped. If this nice lady's priest tells her that cloning is immoral, you can bet that she will stand with the president who believes the same thing.

Religion, God, supernature, superstition, too often stand in the way of human progress in understanding the realities of nature, including self. Once we understand human nature, we humans will be able to appreciate and help our natural fellows in a truly democratic fashion without preying on them. Most humans are by nature good and healthy, not bad and sinful. Nevertheless, it is helpful to patiently bear in mind that because of the strength of these counterproductive traditions, progress comes slowly (for me as well as you). What we, as a species, learned early on in pre-scientific centuries, was imprinted deeply and is difficult to unlearn; similarly, what we, as individuals, learned early on in our pre-rational days, was imprinted deeply and is difficult to unlearn. So be patiently tolerant as you help your neighbor.

DOMESTIC TERROR
ANOTHER BUNION ON THE FOOT OF PROGRESS

We are all part of nature, so we have more natural commonalities between us than differences. However, when one group insists "We Are Right" because we believe the truth and have God on our side, WAR is too often the result. There will likely be terrorism as long as one believing group believes itself superior to the rational guidelines of nature. As long as the "supernatural" and better-than-thou group believes it is the instrument of a just or punishing God, there will always be *jihads* against the infidels, those who believe differently. The general observance of the mutually respectful and reasonable Golden Rule will be postponed further as the representatives of God consider themselves above merely natural human beings.

I am not writing primarily about Middle Eastern *jihads* or terrorism now; I write to point to the danger of fanatical Christian terrorism in America. I forget who it was who said that "good people do good things, and bad people do bad things; but for good people to do bad things, that takes religion." Not always, of course, but too often true. Witness the murders and bombings by anti-abortionists calling themselves The Army of God. The psychological reasons for this are easy to find.

Good-willed folk, truly good people, often believe without questioning. They believe with a deep faith. This is the acceptable way of true faith as shown by a bumper-sticker in the U.S. Bible Belt: "God said it—I believe it—That settles it!" Such an unquestioning believer readily gets fully convinced that his beliefs and those of his minister or his good book are not to be questioned by anyone. He feels he must believe in his true way or he will go to hell, and his reason cannot reign supreme over his feelings. Such deep credulity may not be as common as in bygone days, but we still find many in our midst encouraging everyone to ask WWJD, What Would Jesus Do? Others might ask WWMD, What would Mohammed or Moses do?

When such a believer tries to get others to believe as he does,

I sometimes wonder if he is really trying to help others "get right with God" or to shore up his own wobbly faith. It may only be my perception, but it appears to me that the above bumper-sticker theologians feel they need the crowd-effect of fellow-believers to reinforce their own belief system. In numbers there is often security. "Honk if you love Jesus." (Chapter two discussed the important dynamics of this getting comfort from crowds.)

When the faith system of the more zealous or fanatical believer is directly challenged, one cannot always expect a rational reaction. Keep in mind that the true believer believes in spite of what he actually knows. Faith does not need evidence; faith is founded in the will, not the intellect. So "a man convinced against his will is of the same opinion still." An enthusiastic believer whose faith system is challenged by reason or law can feel so threatened and insecure that he becomes defensive, angry and personally offended. Then he may strike back or react in a dangerously irrational or panicky way. Faith-based terrorism can result.

Tradition-bound groups who attribute infallibility or near infallibility to "our forefathers" or one of their books frequently fail to grow in knowledge and wisdom of the present real world. They remain ill informed and become dangerously dogmatic as they fight to preserve the old beliefs and ways. Such group strength can achieve marvelous goals, both productive and counterproductive. Responsible citizens of the world try to recognize which groups help and which groups hinder humanity's march toward fuller understanding and enjoyment of this world.

Most civilized nations recognize, for example, that no matter how royal the family, there is no longer a "divine right of kings." When this long tradition, earlier accepted by the majority, was found to be counterproductive, the group hypnotic spell was broken. The divine emperor was discovered to have no clothes. Kings and emperors alike have been discovered generally to be merely human. So many customs of long standing have given way to more reasonable approaches to human governance, and the tendency toward cooperative democracy has resulted.

The growth process often proves tedious and difficult, because comforting traditions embraced in pre-rational days die hard. So, I repeat, try to be patient with yourself and others on our journey to finding a better way.

Humankind needed centuries to gradually progress from Greco-Roman and other polytheism and perceived dependency on many Gods to monotheism! Have you ever smiled to yourself as you realize that monotheistic Christians are really atheists less one? They reject the many Gods of Greece and Rome as they hold onto just one. True atheists reject just one more than the monotheists reject. Will it take so long to progress from continuing dependency-engendering monotheism to the independence and self-responsibility of non-theism or atheism? The hypnotic spell of the longitudinal and latitudinal crowds must eventually break. When this spell broke for me, it was like the sun coming up in my life. Meantime, for anyone without some practical knowledge of the marvelous natural power of hypnosis and the resulting natural power of prayer (see Chapter two), it remains understandable why so many still might believe they can access a Higher Power beyond themselves.

The ever-increasing rate of progress in human knowledge furnishes reason for hope. At the same time, however, witnessing the gross amounts and kinds of superstition accepted still today makes one wonder. I wonder how long it will take to break the hypnotic spell of wishful thinking that keeps popes, patriarchs, cardinals, bishops and priests trying to drive out evil spirits by burning candles and incense, sprinkling holy water, or going through other complex liturgies of appeasement.

When I was a youngster, I never questioned such rites; they just were. And for many they still are. In fact, I think most priests and preachers, most ministers and mullahs probably believe some of "supernatural truths" they preach. I think their faithful congregations believe far more of those supernatural preachments than the religious leaders themselves.

So you may wonder, as I do, when those Americans who may

be called right-wing or ultra-conservative of the past will be able to shake off the hypnotic hold of the reverend controllers and realize they can be free, liberated, thinking, joyful human beings. I wonder how long it will take mothers to adequately protect their impressionable youngsters from predatory priests and preying preachers. I wonder when Muslim mothers will break the spell of manipulating mullahs or politically minded clerics and stop them from making murderous martyrs of their children.

Fact-based education, not faith-based tradition, will provide the solution to enslavement of modern minds to latitudinal or longitudinal crowds. Fact-based or scientific education furnishes the most hopeful antidote to popular wishful thinking that convinces millions there are supernatural realities to fulfill their fondest wishes. As educational levels improve, the younger generation may have a less difficult, I did not say easy, challenge to overcome the harmful vestiges of the past.

Educators and scientists have a long and rocky road to travel before overcoming generally the deep prejudices based on one huge counterproductive assumption. The same false assumption pushes the self-proclaimed Army of God (in U.S.) to help their fellow believers kill abortion doctors while lobbying against a pregnant woman's right to choose what she can do with her body.

The problem of a young couple in love (4/2002) demonstrates more subtly how far religious harm can reach. The boyfriend writes desperately to a newspaper counselor for advice: "We are in our late 20s and are serious about each other. Problem is I was born in U.S. and she in Iran. She insists I become Muslim; I'm a Catholic though neither of us is very serious about religion, as such. However, if she tries to travel back to see her family in Iran after marrying a Christian she would be in real danger from the theocratic Iranian government. What can I do without being a hypocrite and joining Islam as she insists?" The 'counselor' answered that she saw no way out of this dilemma. Of course, the dilemma would never have developed if both the lovers had been raised without religion or superstition or the customs based thereon.

The damages from belief-beyond-evidence do not have to be earthshaking to cause great pain. I think no one can estimate to what extent superstitious credulity damages society. The extent of religion's harm is hinted at in the above-mentioned problems of over-population, cheap power and abusive control of non-elected leaders over believers, thousands of divisive and competitive religions, the mental pollution of the naïve, the impediments to ground-breaking medical research, and the public and private terrorism that results when groups of believers dogmatically declare "We Are Right!" But whether the damage is small and subtle or huge and obvious, the counter-productivity of unquestioning religious credulity remains incalculable. Christ is reported to have said, "A good tree cannot bear bad fruit, and a bad tree cannot bear good fruit... By their fruit you will know them." (Matthew 7:18-20)

SEQUITUR/NON SEQUITUR—ACCIDENTAL CREDULITY

A woman and a man are involved in a car accident; it's a bad one. Both of their cars are totally demolished, but amazingly neither of them is hurt. After they crawl out of their cars, the woman says, "So you're a man. That seems interesting. And I am a woman. Wow, just look at our cars! There is nothing left, but we're unhurt. This must be a sign from God that we should meet and be friends and live together in peace for the rest of our days."

Flattered, the man replies, "Oh yes, I agree with you completely!"

"This must be a sign from God!" The woman continues, "and look at this, here's another miracle. My car is completely demolished, but this bottle of wine didn't break. Surely God wants us to drink this wine and celebrate our good fortune." Then she hands the bottle to the man. The man nods his head in agreement, opens it, drinks half the bottle and then hands it back to the woman. The woman takes the bottle, immediately puts the cap back on, and hands it back to the man.

The man asks, "Aren't you having any?"

The woman replies, "No, I think I'll just wait for the police..."

FIVE

GUILT AND RESPONSIBILITY

When I was a young Catholic, I had no idea that perhaps the greatest immorality an adult can curse a child with is to imply to that child that intellectual or logical contradictions are acceptable or possible. In these days of thrilling progress in truly marvelous human achievements, many have concluded that 'anything is possible.' Not true!

Anything that does not imply a logical contradiction is perhaps eventually possible. And even if a star as popular and determined as was Christopher Reeve titles his book *Nothing Is Impossible*, we still must not accept the implication that logical contradictions are possible or acceptable. This would prepare the mind to tolerate a popular immorality that teaches that an innocent child is born in sin, flawed, less good than he ought to be from the very beginning of his life. In a rare news conference, 7/30/03, George W. Bush re-iterated that old Christian teaching: "We are all sinners." Speak for yourself, George, but not for those of us who live true to our logical consciences; and please do not be so illogical as to call an innocent newborn child a sinner in need of rebirth.

RELIGIOUS GUILT CAN UNDERMINE SELF-CONFIDENCE

As a child learning to reason, did you have that ingrained feeling of needing God, grace and forgiveness before you could be whole or good enough? Do you recall, perhaps, as you analyzed the situation a bit later that you should not be held accountable for sins committed prior to your birth? Yet at the intuitive and emotional level, if respected elders taught the need for baptism to wash away your original sin, did you think that, well, they must know what they are doing? So if you were like me in those early developmental days, you likely received the imposed impressions from pre-rational youth that you were somehow guilty and in need of the saving grace and strength of God.

Perhaps other youngsters just missed, ignored or glossed over the meaning of such early Christian lessons. The sensitive, impressionable child who was paying attention could readily see himself as an inadequate and unsatisfactory person. Such a "guilty" person commonly lacks self-esteem.

Low self-esteem causes lack of self-confidence. And a person lacking self-confidence readily gives ear to the manipulative salesmen of questionable programs from drugs to deities. Feeling insufficient and lowly, he feels the need to embrace some power higher than himself. As the naïve and guilty follower with low self-confidence gets cleansed of his assumed sins, he joins the group of the assumed good and godly, and thereby acquires the increased strength of the crowd.

Then, because he cares, he may join the army of those dedicated to helping others see the world as his reinforcing crowd sees it. "After all," says the forgiven believer, "look what religion and God did for me. I was lowly and lost, but now I am found; I was weak, and now I am strong. I was blind, and now I see." The old feeling of personal inadequacy is replaced with a very confident trust in a Higher Power. And the last state of that man may become worse than the first, if, as often happens, his mission now becomes helping others feel as guilty and dependent as he felt before his being forgiven by God. Another Christian bumper sticker comes to mind: "Not perfect, just forgiven." This brings us to the important matter of guilt and responsibility.

PERSONAL RESPONSIBILITY

The notion of an individual taking full, personal responsibility for his actions and their consequences is not overly popular today. Often it appears that no "reasoning" is too fuzzy, no excuse is too flimsy in attempts to duck or lessen personal responsibility for individual decisions: "I blame the tobacco company for making me smoke their addictive carcinogens; my peers pressured me into getting drunk; the car company caused me to drive too fast; my parents gave me bad genes (I'm not really over-weight, I'm under-tall); my teachers didn't care for me; prejudice took away my opportunities; I belong to a disadvantaged minority group; I didn't know the fast food company heated their coffee hot enough to scald me; I didn't even know their hamburgers had fat in them." (Those of you who do not resort to excuses like these may feel the necessity to buy insurance protection against those who do.)

Most preachers would *claim* that mature personal responsibility is a high virtue. Is it fair, then, to wonder why those same preachers do not see that their teachings of guilt, prayer and reliance on the gift of free divine grace can actually help many believers find more ways to duck personal responsibility? Many religious leaders argue strenuously that it is by faith alone, not by good works, that man reaches salvation; they can quote Saint Paul to prove it to themselves.

Legitimately dependent persons are appropriately less responsible than independent ones. So children are not expected to be as broadly responsible as are adults. Responsibility rests with those able to respond effectively, not with helpless little children. And yet a popular teaching of Christianity holds that "unless you become as little children, you cannot enter the kingdom of heaven." (Matthew 18:3)

This dependency attitude explains how children of God can often avoid responsibility; children dependent on the heavenly Father turn the hard stuff over to him. One of my sisters demonstrates this quite clearly. Though she is not my youngest sister, she definitely looks the youngest. Surely her ability to convince herself that "it's in the hands of God" has lifted a lot of big concerns from her shoulders.

It is easier for the Christian Scientist to pray for God to cure a child's deadly disease than to admit God's impotence or lack of caring by responsibly buying appropriate professional help. It is easier, short term, to pray for a "wayward" or learning impaired child than to work patiently oneself or to purchase appropriate help of others. To those who choose to pray as if everything depends on God and work as if everything depends on themselves I say that one of the efforts is mostly wasted; thinking (conscientious) people do not tolerate such implied contradictions. I would encourage more confidence in oneself and more reliance on personal efforts and the help of trustworthy human beings.

A big portion of modern society still believes that God will save man from himself, wash away his sins and personal inadequacies, cleanse his guilt and deliver him into endless happiness. "All you have to do is believe in the healing grace of your Redeemer!" What a deal! In fact, the very common tendency to wish fulfillment makes it difficult for those who feel personally inadequate to resist such a Santa Claus type deal.

The reality is that a responsible or morally upright human being is neither as low and sinful (without redemption) nor as high and superhuman (with redemption) as common religious doctrine would have us believe. A person is not guilty or lowly just because he is a mere human born in someone's assumed "original sin"; nor is he at the other extreme of being supernatural. Being neither devil nor divinity, every human should find his true, responsible position in nature between those two extreme imagined positions of sinner and saint; a complete human is a *rational animal* who enjoys living responsibly, morally—exercising both his mind (rationality) and his body (animality) vigorously while allowing others to do the same. Those guilt-inducing preachers who may or may not have studied theology should recall a central tenet in Moral Theology: guilt, personal immorality, comes from violating one's conscience. And classic moral theology textbooks properly define conscience as "right reason (not emotion nor tradition) deciding what is appropriate or inappropriate for the moral or responsible person in his real, current circumstances."

As a rational animal, a human being is able to respond to, that is, he is responsible for, what he can control. You and I are responsible for what we can control and only what we can control. The responsibility and guilt problems that religions cause (yes, cause) for society have a twofold basis: religion encourages dependency and inadequate reliance on self or one's own conscience (as defined above); and religion too generally convinces believers that this natural world is not really adequate for complete human happiness. I think that it is in this general area that religion or faith in the supernatural does its greatest and most basic psychological damage.

Even though thoughtful persons can go ecstatic at the natural beauties revealed by microscope and telescope, even though perceptive observers can create infinite beauty out of the pollution in a sunset, even though helping one's neighbor brings deep joy to the human heart, supernatural religions still imply that human beings are incapable of creating their own lasting or adequate human happiness. Can you now begin to think differently as you become able to question their gratuitously asserted basic assumption?

Of course, man cannot attain the mysterious, promised absolute happiness of heaven; it's not real, so it cannot possibly be attained by anyone. But neither is hell real, so it cannot be attained either. The carrot and stick, heaven and hell, are groundless assumptions imagined into existence by storytellers, boasters, hero-worshippers and manipulators of the human spirit. You already know what anyone can reasonably do with groundless or gratuitous assumptions. While the balling dung beetle may feel that warm, comforting bullshit is heaven, the rational, moral, self-responsible person may conclude the converse. Reality is right here right now; enjoy it. *Carpe diem!* Use your time morally, productively, helpfully! This life is not a dress rehearsal for anything later. Nor is it a punishment for anything earlier!

As you allow yourself to get free of guilt for things you cannot control, you will enjoy being more adequately responsible for the things you can control. Your resulting freedom will set you apart from those timid souls who insist "Thou shalt not..." "Thou shalt not eat of the Tree of Knowledge or you will be banished with the other brutes." By the way, the Torah, or Pentateuch, the first five books of the Bible, contains 613 commandments or laws; 365 or 60% of these commands are negative. That's a lot of prohibitions to fuel tremendous guilt down through the Judeo-Christian centuries. But what fantastic control and power those prohibitions give to the rabbis and preachers of the scriptures.

Recall how the same Bible says the same God the Father had his only son killed, crucified, according to his own divine design, then held humankind responsible for Christ's death? This scenario, by the way, does not show God to be a sadist. Rather, it shows that the many Judaic, Israelitic, and Christian writers, translators, transcribers, re-translators and interpreters of the Bible had poor historical records, faulty memories, incomplete linguistic knowledge and greatly creative abilities to improvise, moralize and manipulate. (By the way, if you think the above statement is an exaggeration, just Google the phrase "bible versions." In about 0.01 second you get 3.4 million references! This is BIG business!)

Five decades ago, I sat passively in the pews and classrooms and tolerated bible-based attribution of responsibility. In the mid-1950s, I was not yet ready to deny some responsibility for killing

Christ on the cross, even though Christ was the rabble rousing rebel who blatantly resisted the power of the Roman Empire too vigorously for his own good. So, according to Roman law, he received the quite standard punishment of crucifixion for his rebellion. Modern man taking any responsibility for Christ's act of rebellion 20 centuries ago is even more bizarre than a person of today blaming himself for the now obvious immorality of American Negro slavery two centuries ago.

Let's just take full responsibility for our own acts for which we are, indeed, accountable before the bar of reason. These responsible acts and attitudes of ours include respectfully getting along with fellow human beings; this demands, yes, demands that we apply The Golden Rule in our responsible, guilt free dealings with others. (We will deal more fully with The Golden Rule in a later chapter.)

NO GUILT, NO SHAME, NO BLAME, JUST RESPONSIBILITY

When I was making my living as a psychologist, I enjoyed teaching my clients how they could live responsible lives without guilt, shame or blame. Of course, they brought in problems of real guilt and irresponsibility at times. But in the religious suburban area of my clientele, a disproportionate amount of the guilt was imaginary and not really based on their irresponsibility. Too often their problems were based on clashes of their reason and their faith. So in such cases I confided the details of my clerical background and how I had set aside childhood superstitions; it then seemed a lot easier for them to shuck their felt guilt and make rapid progress toward total self-responsibility.

I never tired of helping these clients develop the personal strength to live reasonably with "no guilt, no shame, no blame— just responsibility." Over the years those phrases became almost a mantra. And I thoroughly enjoyed watching my clients rise from their self-defeating postures of helpless guilt and irresponsibility to take rational responsibility for all the things they themselves could really control, but only for the things they could control. The joy of their newly found rational freedom brought me joy also.

If all of us who care, parents, teachers, bosses, preachers, were to help the young take reasoned responsibility with only reasoned consequences for their own actions without any supernaturally based guilt, shame or blame, I think fewer of our youth would be angry, rebellious or cynical. When authority figures assume a divine or superhuman backing for their authority, most maturing youngsters intuitively recognize there's something seriously wrong with the picture even before they can identify the contradiction involved.

These youngsters may not be articulate or experienced enough to put it in words, but they commonly recognize the hypocrisy of such authority figures and some sort of unfair fallacy in their lives. The fallacy or hypocrisy may anger or confuse them. Then they are more likely to rebel, or, what is worse and much more common, they surrender and allow themselves to accept contradictions without adequate skepticism.

I think the greatest immorality and abuse an authority figure can inflict on a learning mind is the fallacy that it should be able to accept perceived contradictions on faith and without checking the assumptions that produced the contradictions. The maturing, independently thinking adolescent will quite naturally tend to rebel, push the envelope and become skeptical of old ways and beliefs. The credulous one, on the other hand, is more likely to relinquish his or her precious logical reason, remain quite docile and accept the possibility of logical contradictions as part of mental life. What a crime!

Then the easy excuses for ducking personal responsibility can be created; logic has already been set aside and implicitly denied as the superior arbiter of morality or personal responsibility; logic be damned. "Yes, I know I'm overweight, but I wanna watch another hour of TV; I don't like to exercise, and I don't have time now anyway." "Yes, I know The Golden Rule says I should be considerate, but this guy is such a stupid, sinful jerk!" "Yes, I know I should quit smoking, but it's too hard; I'm addicted to whatever the tobacco company put in these cigarettes." "Yes, ... but ..." can easily become the mantra of such deeply wounded thinkers. These find it easier to blame outside circumstances beyond their control than to accept reasoned responsibility for life's controllable details—the responsibility that obviates guilt and gives birth to mature self-esteem, legitimate self-confidence and responsible self-control.

HOW TO PROTECT THE CHILDREN

I am confident you know that a child's sense of responsibility is based on his sense of his own self-worth. That self-worth is most precious for any child at the foot of the ladder of success. The question now becomes what to tell the children. How can you help your children become responsible, guilt-free, happy citizens of the world without overwhelming them? "What must the children be told?" It would be too easy to answer the question with one or two words: the truth, facts, just the exciting facts of life. Some expansion of that simple truth may be helpful.

Dependent children need the stable realization that they are safe and that they are loved and respected, valued; they need this perhaps more than any one thing beyond basic bodily nourishment. The naturally curious, creative and exploring child will grow in self-confidence if he knows he can safely trust parental or authority figures. Parents are powerful people, and responsible parents use that great power thoughtfully.

Responsible parents and parental figures know that their actions and attitudes will be learned and imitated without much reasoned censorship by the immature child. So parental values pass on to the younger generation whether the parents like it or not. "Give me the child until he's three; you can have him for the rest of his life; I'll have already formed his *general* attitudes." The psychiatrist who made the above statement exaggerated, but not as much as some parents seem to think.

PARENTAL RESPONSIBILITY

The absence of reliable society-sponsored protection against mental or spiritual pollution of the young leaves the very heavy responsibility for reasoned mental purity and wise value formation primarily with parents. Parents have the first, most effective, and longest lasting influences on their children's values and attitudes. Children come to the world through the parents, and much of the world comes to the children through the parents. It will only be years later, when the children are able to think independently, that old parental ways will likely be challenged. But even during the growthful stages, when maturing youngsters challenge the values of their parents, many of the ingrained prejudices from childhood are likely to remain influential.

If parents act on the prejudices and superstitions they themselves acquired from their own parents, their children will probably grow up nearly as prejudiced as were their parents and grandparents. Can you appreciate now the fact that this is why faiths commonly tend to run in families—right along with other strong family customs, prejudices or traditions?

Prejudice results from forming opinions and making judgments that are not fact-based. Such prejudice or prejudgment can apply to matters of race, religion, family customs, social position or whatever. Reaching a judgment or mental conclusion without examining the pertinent facts is prejudice of some sort. Parents are expected to, are obliged to supply facts (not confusing mysteries and contradictions) to the uninformed minds of their children. But don't worry, parents; just do your reasonable best, your conscientious best. The maturing youngsters will tend to recall your caring efforts even as they grow up and challenge some of your specific teachings and beliefs.

I don't think any conscientious parent would deliberately instill prejudice or fallacies in a child's mind. Thoughtful answers may be difficult, but they are better than too facile answers based on worn out prejudices or superstitions of past generations. The pertinent facts, the truth, will free you from further "lies" and future backpedaling with the child. Later the maturing child, beginning to think more independently, will never have to call you hypocrite, liar or stupid, even as they disagree with you or grow beyond where you were when they were very young.

Of course, children do say the darnedest things and ask about wild and deep subjects. Sometimes they need help with the timing of their questions. Sometimes parents don't know the answer to satisfy the questioning young mind. "I don't know; let's try to find out..." may often be the best, factual answer to a child's boundless and beautiful curiosity. Rarely will a child not deserve a truthful or factual answer; never does a child have a right to a wrong or false answer. The immature child may not be able to handle the whole truth now, but he does have a right to nothing but the truth. Facing up to this parental duty can at times be very challenging.

A mother and her young son were flying on a major airline from Kansas City to Chicago. The son turned to his mother and asked, "If big dogs have baby dogs and big cats have baby cats, why don't big planes have baby planes?" The mother (who couldn't think of an answer that would not lead to items she was not prepared to discuss with her still-too-young son) told him to ask the flight attendant. So the boy did so: "If big dogs have baby dogs and big cats have baby cats, why don't big planes have baby planes?" The flight attendant responded, "Did your mother tell you to ask me?" The boy admitted that this was the case. "Well then, tell your mother that there are no baby planes because our planes always pull out on time. Your mother can explain it to you."

A lie, a piece of misinformation, prejudice, or superstition presented as fact, coming from trusted parental figures, can have long-term negative effects on an impressionable child. The most obvious effect is that a mind's storehouse of knowledge has been contaminated with a fallacy. Any fallacy that is not consistent with the other "facts" in that storehouse will help undermine the self-confidence and self-esteem of the believer of that fallacy. Any parental lie that the child later learns to be a lie will tend to loosen the child's bond of trust in the parents.

If that trust is violated once by parents, the child can reasonably expect it to be violated again. "If they lied to me once, how can I trust that this current answer is not another lie? If they lied to me in the past, why not now about drugs, sex, integrity or guilt? So why should I trust them? Am I not worthy of reliable parents? If I can't depend on my parents, can I believe them when they say they love me? Maybe I'm not worthy of their love."

Self-esteem based on the reality of parental respect for their children is one of the strongest attributes parents can help children develop. If children do not doubt their knowledge of facts gained from loving, caring, respectful parents, they are much more likely to develop the independent self-confidence to deal appropriately with the fallacies, myths and bullshit sales pitches coming later from others who only want to manipulate or use them. Part of parental obligations includes helping children to think critically, to analyze stated "facts" and to discover the real facts of life.

Some of you may be tempted to react to such a call for fact-based honesty by calling it boring, unimaginative, and limiting. Well, what should be more thrilling, the amazing facts of astronomy or the superstitious fantasies of astrology? The prodigious fertility and resurrection of nature in springtime or the fantasy of an egg-laying Easter Bunny? The wonders of generous love delivering whatever the hearts of valuable children need or a fantastic Santa setting them up for broken dreams? The skeptical challenges of science or the mental laziness of credulity. "Thou shalt not eat of the Tree of Knowledge (*scientia*, science)." (Genesis 2:17)

I would hope that parents who succeed in setting aside prejudices of old will be able to rejoice deeply as their self-confident children naturally grow beyond what previous generations had to offer. Such successful parents will surely rejoice as they appreciate their self-confident children standing on their parental shoulders and seeing farther and more clearly than they themselves had been able to see. This is very evident in my large family.

IMPLICATIONS FOR CULTURAL SHARING

Parents today are generally smarter than their own parents. Happily this development takes place very naturally. Societies and individuals learn from one another as the human race gets older and more experienced. This syncretic adaptation of old theories, "facts" and beliefs to new insights, discoveries and experiences happens quite naturally. This evolution is necessary if the human race is to become more human, more rational, as we progress from generation to generation.

Transferring the good parts of your cultural heritage to your children is important. But if you pass your complete cultural heritage to your children unchanged and unimproved, you fail to help them see realities more clearly than you or their grandparents. If you pass on myths and mysteries, pass them on as myths and mysteries, not as facts. I find it instructive to note how some overly proud native and ethnic groups insist on preserving their cultural heritage almost totally intact. They sometimes concentrate on the traditions of the past with such reverence, with so much time and energy, that they seem unable to improve their present situation much beyond that of their ancestors. Thus, their old narrowness, prejudices, myths, superstitions and animosities continue generation after generation right along with their enriching traditions.

Please don't mistake me; a sense of history is very important. One basic reason humankind has been able to progress so far is that we humans learn from the successes and failures of the past. With an appreciative sense of history, we learn to accept the truths and reject the fallacies of the past. We hold on to the things that produce human joy and reject those things that confuse and cause sorrow.

With such a sense of history and caring for both the present and the future, I would insist that naïve children have no right to lies. If persuasive evangelists say their God allows terrible things to happen because of America's sins, tell the impressionable kids why these purveyors of guilt so distort facts. Televangelists, no matter how rich and famous, must not be allowed to get away with the manipulative lying that said that guilty America deserved the terrorist attacks of 9/11/01. These attacks were certainly not God's punishments unleashed on some 2800 men, women and children, even though such fallacious rantings serve to pull in more guilt-offerings from the credulous. If Father Fabrizius is teaching out-dated myths to gullible children, responsible parents help their children sort fact from fiction. Whatever is factual is what children have the right to learn from caring parental figures. The resulting confidence will allow the curious children to never be afraid of facts. Thus they are unlikely ever to fear developing their imaginations endlessly as they deal freely and creatively with life's marvelous and seemingly boundless real wonders.

THE MOST IMPORTANT
OF THE TEN COMMANDMENTS FOR PARENTS

One of the famous Ten Commandments, the eighth or ninth, depending on who's doing the listing, says "Thou shalt not bear false witness." By the way, Christ only mentioned five of the big ten commandments as being necessary for salvation; this one of "not bearing false witness" was his number four (Mt.19:18). This commandment that forbids lying is surely the *most important* one for parents; parental lying to impressionable children is strictly out of bounds.

Lots of parents might say the fourth or the fifth commandment, "Honor thy father and mother," is the most important. Don't worry, parents, the children will honor you if you never bear false witness to them! They may not be able to deal with the whole truth, but these trusting youngsters always have the right to expect nothing but the truth, as you see it, from trustworthy parents. If you parents, and teachers too, never use a lie or a mystery or superstition to avoid telling your youngsters nothing but the truth, the pertinent facts, as you understand them, your mind and theirs will be free to explore more and more of the exciting facets of this marvelous and wonder-filled world of nature.

If you parents and parental figures, do not fear truth and facts, most likely your children will not be afraid of truth and facts. As a result of growing up without fear of facts, they will possess the self-confidence to develop their creativity as they freely pursue ever further the marvelous realities of this wonderful world. As confident citizens, comfortably at home in this real world, they will probably not be afraid to look at any and all the facts with an unpolluted, logical mind. They will fearlessly view reality whether they are seeing the microcosm through a microscope, looking at the obvious through their clear, naked eyes or observing the mind-boggling macrocosm with a spectroscope. Such unpolluted minds will not be afraid to face any of the facts of life. Nor will they be afraid to reject old "facts," when they learn they are no longer facts. This is the scientific method of finding truth.

Hopefully all adults and authority figures will see the practical wisdom of shucking off all undeserved guilt, both for themselves and their immature charges. Then reasoned responsibility based on self-respect will become the rule rather than the exception.

I hope you don't let your youngsters grow up to feel that someone who thinks logically and creatively simply provides a nice contrast to the real world! You self-confident authority figures, forming youngsters without guilt, shame or blame, contribute infinitely to the betterment of society when you teach the facts and demonstrate the truth as you know it. Since you can likely teach the truth better than your parents could, your charges will become able to do it even better than you can. Enjoy this most important responsibility without guilt.

SEQUITUR/NON SEQUITUR—PERSONAL

Last night, after putting the penultimate touches on this Chapter Five, I retired at about my regular time. And I had a dream that I was going to confession. Now I have not been in a confessional, on either side of the screen (except as a tourist), for over thirty-five years. Nevertheless, the dream had a jumble of details in it that were pretty reminiscent of some of old realities. (That's what I had been writing and thinking about, so no surprise.)

The setting was in a large church; it could have been Holy Angels in Aurora, Illinois, where I helped the padres there with their pastoral work at various times. The church was crowded; mass was about ready to start on Sunday morning. In examining my conscience as I prepared to make my confession, I was having trouble coming up with something of substance to tell to the priest.

As the priest approached the confessional to hear my confession, he seemed to be starting something like the dance of the seven veils, and then I started my confession ritual: "Bless me, father, … it's been a week, maybe two, I'm not sure, since my last confession…" I mentioned being unkind a time or two, as I recall the dream, and that's about how it ended.

I am not making this stuff up; it happened last night. And I share it with you, because I know from both my pastoral and psychological practices that many people become superstitious and put far too much value on dreams and sometimes get upset or believe the impossible as a result. Some use dreams as prophecies or interpret them as evidence of their personal clairvoyant powers and so forth. Dreams have been interpreted (generally extremely over-interpreted) down through history in a multitude of ways and for various reasons. Sometimes they have been used to influence history. Dreams have contributed to many of the prophecies and other stories in the Bible. Similarly, Freud grossly over-interpreted dreams and their importance.

The basic thing to recognize about a dream is that it can grab subject matter from absolutely any previous experience of the dreamer, whether old or recent, whether real or imagined, whether desired or dreaded. Then any of these elements can be jumbled or combined in any manner whatsoever, simply because the logical censor is asleep. While the logical watchman is asleep, the subconscious can run totally wild.

So, when you are fighting your battles with the past and working to get free to grow beyond that less mature past, please don't let dreams of any sort slow your conscious pursuit of truth or reality; they are not reliable contributors to productive thought processes.

SIX

FAITH CAN LEAD TO
EXTREMES

Many decades ago, when I was still in the minor seminary, I enjoyed a memorable book appropriately titled *Enthusiasm*. Odds are it is no longer in print. Its main thesis was that over-enthusiasm for any dogmatic position can cause a person to lose reliable grounding in objective reality; the results can become pretty absurd. As I recall that book, I now appreciate how it must have influenced me far more deeply and positively than I realized at that time.

In the previous chapter we dealt with guilt and reasoned responsibility in such a way as to be able to live without guilt, shame or blame. It is time now to look at how faith sometimes goes far beyond reason's boundaries in counter-productive ways. However, in the following discussion of such extremes, it will repeatedly become important to make deliberate efforts to appreciate differing points of view.

It is pretty easy for both you and me to see our own points of view so clearly that it becomes just as easy to ignore or depreciate an opposing point of view. It will be helpful to bear in mind then that opinions are freely held as mere opinions. It is, therefore, very easy to disagree with another's freely held opinion; you may readily challenge my opinions, and I may debate yours. But though we may strenuously disagree with each other's opinions, I hope we can consistently respect each other's right to the differing opinion when honestly expressed.

This matter of mutual respect brings to mind an impressive billboard I saw in my recent continental travels. This billboard was impressive for its imposing size and placement along a busy freeway, but it was far more impressive for its simple message: **"COURTESY AND RESPECT**—Don't worry, you'll get used to it." Isn't that a nice way to encourage observance of The Golden Rule in dealing with matters of personal opinion and faith? Let us both try to keep sight of it as we observe some of the extremes that faith can lead to.

For the believer, faith is understandably above reason. I myself functioned for some thirty years assuming my faith to be superior to reason. So when my youthful faith and reason were in conflict, faith won over reason. Current observation of dedicated believers as well as repeated biblical references indicate that the true believer does not waver or quit believing merely because reason challenges. "Faith exceeds all knowledge and all understanding," so, according to St. Paul, true faith never falls away.

A half century ago America, in her fight against atheistic communism, got caught up in a McCarthyism that tended to find a communist in every shaded corner of American life. The believers in that McCarthyism, in their enthusiastic attack on atheistic communism, concluded that "extremism in the defense of virtue is no vice." This sounded good to a lot of believers until it became obvious that many U.S. citizens were being deprived of their rights because they were merely suspected of having communist sympathies. Most reasonable Americans soon lost faith in such extremism and abandoned McCarthyism.

Very few Americans had gotten so hooked on McCarthyism that they could not abandon their faith in it when they saw how it threatened their personal freedoms. It was too extreme for most level-headed Americans. Though McCarthyism showed briefly how belief in a fallacy can lead to extremism, it did not last long enough to become traditional; there was very little longitudinal crowd influence; so it never reached the point of becoming a self-perpetuating addictor for American society.

CAN RELIGION BECOME THE OPIATE OF THE PEOPLE?

As we prepare to consider a few extremes that some supernatural beliefs lead to, and as we realize how drug addicts go to extremes to get their fixes, we may discover how Karl Marx was correct when he called religion the opium of the people. Can religion serve to control the masses and "keep them down on the farm" to such an extent that they do not have adequate drive to throw off the shackles of past traditions and beliefs that are no longer helpful?

Consider the dealer of addictive drugs. He finds someone who has a problem—an easy task. The pusher offers an easy solution, free at first, like grace, until his victim becomes drug dependent; then the price of the drug gradually becomes so burdensome that the addict becomes another pusher in order to satisfy his own craving. He finds another imperfect human being who is needy enough to believe the new pusher's pitch of cheap power and easy escape from personal problems; so the cycle of dependency is repeated as addicts beget more addicts.

This is the vicious cycle of dependency on cheap power or phony strength that comes from outside oneself rather than from within the self. This self-propagating cycle of dependency catches millions of self-dissatisfied individuals who put their trust in a destructive, addictive drug that promises them deliverance from their trials and tribulations.

How is this cycle of self-perpetuating addiction so different from humankind's traditionally widespread dependence on religions or Gods of many sorts for eons?

Let us suppose a person, anyone, happens to have low self-esteem or a feeling of self-inadequacy. A preacher, shaman, or any purveyor of superhuman strength says, "Yes, you are just a weak human being, a sinner unless and until you embrace my redemptive religion." If this person with low self-esteem becomes a new believer and is given grace, forgiveness and redemption, he believes he has now become more than merely a weak human being. Consequently he now feels more adequate; he feels good even without dealing with his personal inadequacy problems. He gains in self-confidence and personal strength as he is reinforced by the gang of believers.

As he becomes more and more a "true believer," he becomes more and more convinced that his religion or God is the one true one, the solution to his problems, the source of his strength and fulfillment. Now, since he is a good person who cares, he also wants others to share his faith system. So he, in turn, becomes the new promoter, preacher or missionary who wants to feed the hungry sheep and show them the way to the feeling of peace and superhuman strength. And the beat goes on! It seems clear that Rev. Franklin Graham will continue seamlessly the repetitive message of his popular, aging father, Rev. Billy Graham.

This beat is easy to follow, very attractive, because it responds so well to man's almost universal and natural desire for more—always more, never totally satisfied until we get more: more power, more speed, more money, more grace, more friends, more knowledge, more health, more security, more possessions, more pleasure, more wisdom and on and on. This commonly felt need for more drives the curious and scholarly to greater efforts to resolve the mysteries of ignorance; but it convinces others (the majority?)

that natural human beings must have supernatural help to enjoy adequate fulfillment or complete happiness.

Religion recognizes man's very commonly perceived self-inadequacy, and it furnishes an antidote to that feeling. Those many who believe they have been saved and lifted up by superhuman power now march to the beat of a divine drummer; and being good-willed people, they often insist that we all become good people in their eyes. The true believers, those who really believe they ought to help God make the world better, often go beyond quiet personal lives to become messengers of God, missionaries or enlistees in the Armies of God to fight the crusades and *jihads* for an all-powerful God.

The deeper and more totally the drug addict believes in the value of the savior substance that aggravates his dependence, the more hurtful he becomes to himself and perhaps even to society. The addict's denial of his problem may be so complete that he commonly puts himself beyond society's helping efforts. Is it possible that the same could be said for true or fundamental believers, those who believe in the need for supernatural help and guidance to find human happiness? I think so, for I was in that group for well over two decades. I believed so strongly and deeply that I was beyond the reach of the helping hand of the commonsense world. I was clearly set on this journey of credulity by my early unquestioning acceptance of parental traditions, and I was thrilled as I thought I possessed a superhuman power based on that credulity.

It wasn't so very long ago that almost everyone believed the earth was flat, assumed it so. The Catholic Church insisted dogmatically that the earth was the flat center of the whole universe, because God had sent his only son to specially redeem this earthly world. And yet, once that traditional and almost universally accepted flat-earth assumption was shown to be false, astronomical progress quickly resulted. When good people reach bad (counterproductive) conclusions, re-examine the assumptions! When our own beliefs encourage us to act irrationally, inconsistently, disrespectfully, immorally, discourteously or irresponsibly, we need to check our assumptions or beliefs. Let the opiate buyer beware! *Caveat emptor; caveat creditor!* Let the believer beware!

Supernatural believers feel, as I did for so long, that they are the ones who know God's will. So those who would "lead us not into temptation" readily become moral policemen and judges of what is good or evil, whether reasonable or not. Consider all of their caring, their background, their traditions, their assumptions and perhaps *especially* their vested interests; then it will be much easier to understand their position. But in order to avoid reaching unreasonable extremes with them, verify their assumptions before following them to any extreme faith-based conclusions.

FROM ENTHUSIASTIC EXTREMES TO ALARMING ABSURDITIES

The following are a few examples of what I see as extreme conclusions reached by enthusiastic believers today. Christian Science parents and others watch their children die for lack of scientific medical treatment while they pray for God to save the innocent children. Exorcisms are performed as in the Dark Ages of Faith instead of getting the sufferer adequate psychiatric help. Pope John Paul II, when asked about his performance of three exorcisms during his papacy, would not deny that he had tried the old liturgical efforts to drive the devil(s) out of the sick. And the Vatican under Pope Benedict XVI more recently published detailed directions as to how priests should conduct exorcisms to drive devils from supposedly possessed human beings.

Abortion doctors are murdered, because God's self-appointed representatives, The Army of God, decided it's better to rid society of abortion doctors, mature, tax-paying family men, than to help responsible adults get rid of zygotes, unwanted neoplasms, or unformed or malformed fetuses with far, far less actual human rights. Such self-appointed representatives of God believe that God creates an immortal soul, making a human being, a new human person, at the very moment of fertilization (two cells). This conception, they say, immediately produces a new human being with full rights. They fail miserably to make the distinction between what is potentially a human being and what is actually a human being. (If potential and actual were the same, would we all be wise, loving, and happy multi-millionaires?)

If human conception produces a human, does chicken conception produce a chicken? When these believers crack open their breakfast eggs and find some of them had obviously been fertilized, are they now having chicken for breakfast? How many chickens can a conservative Christian eat for breakfast, especially when the egg has twin fertilized yolks? Years ago when it was a mortal/deadly sin for Catholics to eat meat on Friday, should they have thrown away those young chickens discovered to be hiding among the eggs on Friday morning? This is not really such a trivial matter at all when you realize that probably as many as one-half to three-fourths of fertilized human eggs never implant; they end as "spontaneous" or natural abortions, miscarriages or unnoticed human events. Now, if these fertilized ova are really human beings with rights, how do you think the conservative Christians should deal with all those millions of non-funerals?

The free assumption by enthusiastic conservative Christians that God breathes a valuable, immortal soul into a couple of cells and makes them an actual human being at the very moment of conception is what motivates them to take such an extreme stance regarding the sacredness of human conception. (As one very vulgar wag put it, "Given this assumption, any lowly mother-fucker can control God; he can force God's consent to create, whether the potential mother consents to the creation or not!!!") Enthusiastic acceptance of this basic, unproven assumption blinds such believers to the obvious and suspends their common sense. Once a mind, polluted by illogic, believes one mystery, it becomes more capable of believing other mysteries or contradictory assumptions.

REPEATED FALLACIES BECOME BELIEVABLE
Successful politicians are not the only ones who have long known

that if a myth is repeated often enough, more and more people will come to believe it. The pushers of myths realize very well that you can fool some of the people all the time. In our hurried society, very little history, theology and philosophy are studied today. Therefore, it is easier for many moderns to believe traditional myths, superstitions and "matters of the spirit" than to study, analyze and question them. In order to be true to our rational selves, when myths or traditions, whether they come from the Bible, the pulpit, parents or the horoscope, prejudice us in any way, we owe it to ourselves to evaluate those old assumptions carefully. If any of these sources asks us to set reason aside, we need to examine that source very carefully for its reliability and real productivity.

We have been told very often about a good, loving and just biblical God. At the same time, if we believe the many authors of the Bible, the God of that Bible commands and helps with genocide over and over, punishes whimsically, vengefully and incredibly severely. This God leaves blood on battlefields and doorposts to prove his protection. *Jihads* of so many types continue in the name of God that a reasonable person may justifiably wonder if trying to do the will of such a God is productive.

Over and over again, from the assumed original sin onward, the Bible comes down hard on knowledge seekers. Scientists want to know, not just believe; responsible humans want to verify, not just trust. It is understandable that the Bible would seem unscientific by modern standards; but it is anti-scientific as well. "Thou shalt not eat of the Tree of Knowledge!" was one of the very first commandments to Adam and Eve. To me it seems legitimate to wonder if this was Moses trying to keep the Jews "down on the farm" for control purposes rather than anything from the mouth of a wise God.

More modern faith-based extremes will be discussed a bit later.

SEQUITUR/NON SEQUITUR—SALESMANSHIP

The kids filed back into class on Monday morning. They were very excited. Their weekend assignment had been to sell something, then give a talk on productive salesmanship.

Little Mary led off: "I sold Girl Scout cookies, and I made $30," she said proudly. "My sales approach was to appeal to the customer's civic spirit, and I credit that approach for my obvious success."

"Very good," said the teacher.

Little Sally was next. " I sold magazines," she said, "I made $45, and I explained to everyone that magazines would keep them abreast of current events."

"Very good, Sally," said the teacher.

Eventually, it was the preacher's son, Johnny's turn. Teacher held her breath.

Little Johnny walked to the front of the classroom and dumped a box full of cash on the teacher's desk. "$2,467," he said.

"$2,467," cried the teacher, "what in the world were you selling?"

"Toothbrushes," said little Johnny.

"Toothbrushes," echoed the teacher, "how could you possibly sell enough toothbrushes to make that much money?"

"I found the busiest corner in town," said little Johnny, "I set up a Chip and Dip stand. I gave everybody who walked by a sample. They all said the same thing. 'Hey, this tastes like shit!' Then I would say, 'It is shit. Wanna buy a toothbrush?'"

PATRIOTIC EXTREMES

It's disappointing to observe how the post 09/11/01 patriotic surge was connected to a surge in public religiosity. Quite naturally when a person's country is attacked (especially with such a horrible wake-up call as on 09/11/01), citizens who love the country will show greater manifestations of patriotism. However, in a pluralistic country like the U.S., with a large number of nontheistic patriotic citizens, it seemed a bit absurd to note how some religionists used the increased patriotism after that 09/11/01 debacle to try to change our national anthem from "The Star Spangled Banner" to "God Bless America." If such an effort were to succeed, it should be considered another instance of tyranny of the majority over the minorities.

IN GOD WE TRUST

When the U.S. treasury first put the motto, "In God We Trust," on hard U.S. currency (1864), the country was still fighting its bloodiest and most desperate Civil War. Millions of fathers, brothers and sons had already spilled each other's blood in the most disgraceful and wasteful conflict in United States history. One might understand the desperation of the treasury officials who felt they couldn't trust the currency without some supernatural help back in those dark days nearly a century and a half ago.

In far less desperate times, a Congress with its finger in the wind and ignoring the wisdom of Jefferson, Adams and Paine, resolved in 1956 that "In God We Trust" become our national motto. That same motto appeared on our paper currency a year later. To what purpose, if not religious? Does the currency with the motto buy more because it carries a religious slogan? Is it a more reliable currency? And does it belong to the State or God? "Render to Caesar the things that are Caesar's."

I was surprised to read of a school superintendent in Jacksonville, FL, saying that if putting this motto, "In God We Trust," in the schools can help build patriotism, it has served its purpose. So State sponsorship of slogans promulgating the God assumption is justified because it seems to increase patriotism? Is God an American or a nationalist of any kind? Or is it more likely that religious enthusiasts will grab onto most any vehicle, constitutional or not, to subtly inculcate their ideas? Is it excusable for that Florida public educator, in the beginning of the twenty-first century, to use such bumper-sticker theology for sectarian purposes? Can you agree with my opinion that students in pluralistic public schools in America have a right to more constitutional respect?

I receive preachy e-mails that imply a person ought to believe in God in order to show patriotism. "America, love it or leave it; our motto is 'In God We Trust,' and if you don't like it, leave," say these zealots. But I like America's original United States motto much more: "*E pluribus unum*" (From many one—From many peoples one people—From many states one country).

This *E pluribus unum* is the motto that truly describes America with her open arms accepting and enfolding all good-willed comers. And if you don't like that original motto, don't leave; let's work together to understand each other and unite us rather than divide us. "In God We Trust" more aptly describes far less successful sectarian theocracies.

Could this zealous push for motto-changing be interpreted as just another insidious way to help brainwash the unwary into continuing the assumption that there is a God? This bumper-sticker motto (In God We Trust) appears to be growing in popularity. In an attempt to make it appear constitutionally acceptable as a motto for our pluralistic society, however, one outrageously wish-fulfilling politician said "It is secular. It's not a religious statement, and it's something we should be proud of—it's our national motto." (Mich. State Represent, (R) Stephen Ehardt, AP report, 2/28/02). It is secular? Wow, how's that for rationalization or wishful thinking?

In our young American society, we have not yet become theocratic. However, are we racing in that direction as we popularly mix religion and patriotism? "In God We Trust" is supposed now to be our national motto; yet according to two of our most popular Christian televangelists, we were attacked on 09/11/01 because we Americans are sinners who have lost God's protection for not adequately trusting God. Are we really so guilty as a successful human society, or is faith again clouding out reason?

ONE NATION UNDER GOD

The patriotism and allegiance of the generation that won World War II were apparently somehow inadequately expressed. All of us in that generation went through school and the great war pledging a Godless allegiance ("...one nation, indivisible..."); but that was not adequate for the religious manipulators of young minds. So in 1954 politicians again listened to religionists and legislated the modification of our Pledge of Allegiance to include a new religious phrase.

Again the Jeffersonian Wall of Separation between Church and State was breeched with the editing of that beautiful declaration of patriotism. Now all children, believers or not, get to babble "...one nation, under God, indivisible" or be different from the potentially and often actually tyrannical majority.

Nevertheless, in the summer of 2002, a federal judge in San Francisco ruled such use of this religious phrase in the pledge to be unconstitutional in public schools. Loud howls of utter rejection and deep disdain came immediately from the religionists as they seemed to conveniently ignore the Constitution again.

And how did our lawmakers in Congress react? Unanimously, as a herd of sheep, they immediately rushed together to proclaim their allegiance to the flag, literally yelling at the TV cameras that we are "...one nation UNDER GOD! indivisible..." "That erroneous decision in the federal court in San Francisco will be overturned!" cried this congressional crowd in unprecedented unanimity. One might somehow understand the enthusiastic religionists howling as they ignored the Constitution, but all these lawmakers should have had the courage to show that they knew better.

That constitutional decision of the federal judge might indeed be overturned as so many congressional legislators predicted even though it dealt only with our pluralistic public schools. In such event, the impressionable youngsters will continue to be subtly brainwashed into the improbable God assumption even in the public (state) schools. Responsible, thinking parents will then have heightened responsibility to counter such unconstitutional tyranny of the majority over the minority.

FIRST AMENDMENT TO THE CONSTITUTION

The U.S. Constitution was ratified June 21, 1788. Three—and-a-half years later the very First Amendment to that document stated clearly that "Congress shall make no law respecting an establishment of religion or prohibiting the free exercise thereof; ..." In the context of separation of Church and State, some seem to think the First Amendment stops or is complete with the above wording; but this is not so. That First Amendment goes on to say: "... or abridging the freedom of speech, or of the press; or the right of the people peaceably to assemble, and to petition the Government for a redress of grievances." While the Constitution remains free from religion, this same Constitution guarantees freedom of religion and peaceful assembly for all.

Many early settlers came to America to flee state supported religious persecution in their older societies. Often these same "refugees" promptly proceeded to set up their own little theocratic societies in their new world colonies, sometimes resulting in witch hunts, confinement in stocks and even worse. These local theocracies experienced various degrees of religious persecution and social failure during the two centuries before the drafting of the Constitution. This civic or "state" sponsorship of religion and the divisions engendered thereby influenced the founding fathers to be very sensitive to stress that the United States government would not legislate a state religion or sponsor any religion at all. The founding fathers saw clearly what state sponsorship of religion had done both in England and especially in colonial America. So we haven't had a witch burning in a long time.

Likewise the government shall not set aside "... the right of the people peaceably to assemble, ..." All our citizens should be able to exercise their right to assemble peacefully. But when an assembly (religious or not) leads to irrational, counterproductive, or even seditious conclusions, that assembly, reason says, is no longer protected by the Constitution. Any assembly that rouses the rabble or encourages the members to take unreasonable and socially destructive actions must be reined in by reasonable authority. This truth was clearly demonstrated when the U.S. civil courts stepped in to stop the pedophilia that was so widespread in the Catholic Church in the late twentieth century. Such assertion of civil authority over clearly abusive religious authority surely seems appropriate to thinking citizens with the general welfare in mind.

To religionists, however, it sometimes appears to be unacceptable. "We respond to a Higher Power, and the State has no power over this religious assembly. Our God is above your human laws. In serious matters or in frivolous matters, let us alone; let us smoke peyote, pollute the air with incense and candle burning, protect criminal sinners in confession, hide the crimes of pedophiles, pollute young minds with impossible mysteries and logical contradictions, campaign against any politician or civic or scientific project we object to, encourage over-population schemes, plot any obstruction or destruction that helps us fight God's war for more souls. You purely human beings, leave us alone.

"Essentially we are above the discipline of reasoned civil law, because we are supernatural, doing God's will. We will tell you how to get un-guilty and thereby prevent terrorist attacks such as on 09/11/01; don't bother us, don't obstruct us no matter how anti-social or anti-scientific our customs are, just so long as they are religious customs!!" Thankfully, civil authorities finally forced the Catholic Church (in 2002) to quit considering priestly pedophilia outside or above the civil law; a pervasive old religion-protected immorality was finally forced into public view.

Frequently in America a racist or other zealot with an axe to grind will become a minister (with or without education). This role gives the Reverend(?) quick access to cheap power. In America whenever a movement or a person can be tagged religious, great numbers flock to participate. It seems popular faith is insatiable; you can fool some of the people all of the time. So new sects and cults multiply to the embarrassing extent that there are now many thousands of them in the U.S.

CAN IRRATIONALITY BE IMMORAL?

Two impressive and popular preachers, televangelists with great popular power and influence, Reverend Pat Robertson and Reverend Jerry Falwell, on national TV, agreed right after the World Trade Center towers were destroyed on 09/11/01 that God had clearly withdrawn his protective mantle from shielding sinning America. This supposed guilt is why Allah beat God that awful morning killing thousands of men, women and children that most people considered innocent. But these preachers are pros; they learned early in their preachers' training how to first make the audience feel low and guilty. Next, promise to lift them up with Christ's redeeming forgiveness and grace; then make the money pitch and take up the collection.

I have to marvel at how popular these two preachers have become—how much credence masses of Americans seem to put in these men. I personally wonder if these men believe themselves. How could they possibly be as smart as they obviously are in business and political matters and still believe what they seem to expect their contributors to believe? Their popularity is nothing short of marvelous. Is it because they, like many successful religious leaders, are so articulate that they help their listeners hypnotize themselves, suspend rational analysis, set aside all skepticism and uncritically trust their destiny to some supposed Higher Power?

For someone who is overly busy, overwhelmed by sickness in the family, concerned about job security, or anxious about life's daily demands, this can bring a peace that really feels good. For such believers, the teaching of Christian guilt and redemption by a loving savior may help them feel much richer and larger than they can be alone; and then the believers' lives become more worthwhile.

In a somewhat similar fashion, I think many apparently successful moderns, working hard to get more out of life but frustrated at not getting enough to satisfy them, may simply enjoy a relaxed peace as they, like my successful second youngest sister does, "leave all the tough problems in the hands of God."

In Ayn Rand's *Atlas Shrugged* (New American Library, paper, 1957, p. 459), she has her hero stating: "...I think that the only real moral crime that one man can commit against another is the attempt to create... an impression of the contradictory, the impossible, the irrational, and thus shake the concept of rationality in his victim." In other words, Rand saw the undermining of logical functioning of the mind as the greatest possible mental pollution. She wrote this long before Falwell and Robertson had such broad influence. In our pluralistic society, you can find a lot of voters for the Falwell/Robertson approach to personal value and peace; on the other hand, you can find a rapidly growing number of people who would vote for Rand's position. I trust that you can responsibly decide for yourself which group makes more long term sense to you.

I question whether anyone should have the right to try to impress a young or naïve person that he was born in sin or that logical contradictions can actually exist in the real world. The logically impossible is not logically possible! And I would hope that any preacher or parental figure would take conscientious steps to strengthen the rational character of the young minds they influence.

After the 2001 and 2002 discoveries of the widespread epidemic of clergy abusing children physically, the pope and many bishops repeatedly and profusely apologized because "we failed to protect the innocent among us, our children." These clerics apologized for those most despicable and destructive crimes centuries late and only when forced into the open by responsible civil authorities. Should we ever expect their apologies for the more subtle failure to protect the minds, the spirits, of the many millions of naïve and innocent children everywhere? (An interesting lawsuit in Italy has just come to light in 2006. An atheistic attorney is suing the local priest and the Vatican for pushing the myth of the very existence of Christ. The outcome is still unknown.)

Your conscience ("right reason deciding about the appropriateness of this action for you") will surely guide you in deciding whether or not teachers of supernatural mysteries should continue to do so. One's conscience should always be one's guide, and no mysterious experience allows setting it aside. As a person who agrees with Ayn Rand that deliberately undermining the rationality of a human mind is highly immoral, I long for the day when the preachers of imagined guilt admit to their responsibility for weakening the rationality of impressionable minds by teaching contradictory and irrational mysteries.

It took me a long time to reach this personal position; as I admitted earlier, I was a very slow unlearner of the impressive lessons of childhood. One of the main purposes of this book is to undo some of the psychological/spiritual damage I unwittingly did in my youth. Whatever stage of your own development you find yourself in, I hope you enjoy pursuing the dictates of your own conscience and picking your own way to secure personal peace.

I think the math teacher who would try to convince students that three times one is one should not remain a math teacher. I also think that any social studies teacher who deliberately teaches that a person can be guilty just by being born or that human beings are naturally bad should be fired for immoral and irresponsible behavior.

Yet parents and preachers easily pass on cultural heritage as they tell the impressionable about the mysteries of the Trinity (three persons in one simple and changeless God, a changeless God who should be prayed to?). They teach as fact the Virgin Mary's sexless, supernatural conception of the human Jesus. (Many old religions taught similar sexless conceptions before the time of Christ.) They teach that Jesus is the second person of the absolutely simple and eternally perfect, trinitarian God. (How many contradictions can you find in that teaching of the mysterious

Trinity?) They insist that everyone is guilty at birth, so everyone has to get washed by baptism. The sacrament of baptism is the door-sacrament necessary for admission to the society of those who can enter into heaven. This is serious stuff.

Most all of us learned very young that the Santa Claus myth was false. This one was easy to reject, because we could see clear, natural evidence that contradicted the old myth. But you cannot disprove a non-falsifiable **super**-natural myth. Some very perceptive people could reject other mythical and supernatural teachings while young, because they concluded quite early that these mysterious things were not helpful for them. However, others of us needed much more time to reject the mythical, supernatural and mysterious teachings of tradition.

There are several reasons for this more tardy rejection of religious mysteries: the contradictory evidence was not so simple and clear as with the Santa myth; parental figures were more serious and more persevering in their teaching of traditional religious doctrines; the consequences of rejection seemed much more serious especially for those who still believed in hell; and, since faith is a matter of the will, it can over-ride the conclusions of the intellect, no matter how rational those intellectual conclusions are. Depending on your own personal insights and experiences, you can likely think of other personal reasons for delaying your rejection of some of the early religious mysteries.

We develop at different rates. And since we do so, it would be wrong to suggest that a person who sincerely believes he is following his conscience by believing supernatural mysteries is acting immorally. Such a condemnation of the conscientious would be highly unfair. By contrast, however, anyone who hypocritically, insincerely or manipulatively teaches illogical mysteries as though they believed them seems highly immoral to me. (Could Falwell and Robertson be right when they say, "We are sinners"?)

I myself now find it impossible to accept the old religious teaching that humankind is evil by nature. Even President George W. Bush quoted a related religious teaching on national television when he said "We are all sinners." In matters of religion, speak only for yourself, George. Believe it for your personal self, if you must, but I don't want you to further corrupt youthful minds with mysteries that imply that at times it's O.K. to 'think' illogically or irrationally.

Once a young mind is motivated by an apparently credible person to see the irrational as possible, it becomes more capable of believing any set of beliefs without adequate censorship of reason. When reason is suspended, as in dreaming, all kinds of bizarre and disorderly happenings seem real and feasible; then on waking, reason takes over to provide better reality contact. When reason is suspended in order to believe a supernatural mystery, the reality-checking censor is inappropriately allowed to go off duty.

To the extent that the guiding and censoring control of reason is suspended when awake, the likelihood of irresponsible behavior increases. This is so, whether reason's control is weakened by drugs, tiredness, brain damage, emotional disturbance or unrealistic natural or supernatural tenets of faith. Nightmarish behavior can result. For an extreme example, consider how some conservative Christians justify or encourage the bombing of abortion clinics because the murderers believe their mystery that God creates a special immortal soul at the very instant of conception, even if that conception is the result of rape, deception, incest or whatever.

In the past several decades, the youngsters of much of the Middle East have heard repeatedly that they must fight a *jihad* for Allah—Allah not being able, of course, to do his own fighting. Once these brainwashed youngsters abdicate their reason to their faith, they can accept the imagined value of dying while fighting for Allah. So faith-based suicides continue in the name of God. Similar extremes can be found in the interminable Hindu-Muslim conflicts in India and Pakistan. In my opinion, most of these nightmares and dozens of other religio-ethnic wars would likely have faded away long ago if religious teachers, preachers and mullahs had been ignored when they suggested illogical or irrational tenets.

Before 2001 it had been common practice to re-assign pedophilic priests to other parishes and let them continue ministering. By 2002 the civil law began to force more practical methods of dealing with such abusive priests. Their bishops fired them, but only after civil authorities exposed the clerics' crimes and forced the firings.

It may be time for many other firings! It is my own opinion that the preachers of supernatural ghost stories or dreams should be fired. However, you have to decide according to your own conscience when or if you should let them go. I suggest that we let all of them get real jobs; some of them would make pretty good social workers; a huge lot of them would make excellent actors. For me it is time to give more attention to the knowledge seekers, the humble scientists who admit that there are probably no real mysteries, just temporary ignorance of realities, temporary lack of appropriate knowledge which we have to work for.

In this discussion of destructive extremes that supernatural faith sometimes leads to, I have concentrated on threats to human rationality. I have deliberately avoided dealing with the wonderful and transcendent matter of the arts, for this is not an area wherein I have much expertise. I do appreciate the natural enrichment of the human spirit that the natural muses can furnish. Such imaginative, artistic enrichment goes well beyond the capabilities of reason and deeply enriches the purely rational mind without contradicting it. I doubt that Einstein would have contributed so very much to the rational science of physics if he had not enjoyed his relaxing ecstasies with his violin and Mozart.

It is likely that much of so-called religious appeal to the spirit of modern man is due to the rich, but natural, artistic heritage of religions. For example, even after all these post-Christian years, I still catch myself enjoying some of the old Gregorian melodies and other religious hymns. And who could not enjoy many of the wonderful visual beauties of the Vatican, no matter what his or her belief system? These artistic achievements bring enrichment of the human spirit beyond that achievable by reason alone; their natural beauties accomplish this uplift of the human spirit even in spite of the fact that at some logical level they may be offensive because of the contradictory lessons they impart.

FURTHER EXTREMES

Previously described faith-based extremes were found to inhibit independent adult rational functioning. Further questionable developments multiply wonderfully as believers discover divine intervention in their everyday lives.

MIRACLES

On January 4, 2006, front page headlines of many morning newspapers heralded an acclaimed miracle that "12 of 13 miners found alive" after being trapped in a Sago, West Virginia coal mine for over two days. All the hearts of those crowding into the local Baptist church rejoiced ecstatically as they thought their fervent prayers had been answered. One can only imagine the depth of their sorrow and disappointment as they learned two hours later the tragic truth that only one young man was found alive. The lengthy front page article filled in a lot of the details of this "miracle" that turned out to be an almost total tragedy. Obviously newspaper reporters are too often more eager to report miracles than prosaic realities. This is understandable, since it helps sell their copy. However, a healthy skepticism on our part will help protect us from unrealities.

Through the perceived miracles in their mundane existence, believers readily prove to themselves God's loving existence. Indeed, the accepted definition of "miracle" is "a marvelous happening attributed to divine intervention."

A very sincere couple, waiting in the same doctor's office I was in, reported a miracle to me on April 17, 2002. This lady and her husband described enthusiastically how one doctor had examined her carotid arteries and found them to be problem free. Then three days later, after she had traveled a great distance to join family and friends, her doctor called to notify her that her test results had been misread or misinterpreted. He ordered her to hurry back to him for further analysis. The doctor seemed alarmed.

This religious woman prayed hard and immediately enlisted the prayers of her friends and relatives. Then on returning to her doctor, he confirmed that, indeed, she had no problem with her carotid arteries. Both she and her husband declared forcefully that this was a miraculous cure granted in virtue of the prayers. How could anyone attribute something so natural as a diagnostic error to some supernatural power?

Many decades ago, when I was still in the seminary, I learned in logic class that we should accept any feasible natural explanation of a marvelous situation rather than jump to a supernatural explanation. Likewise, we should use a simple explanation when possible, rather than embrace an unnecessarily complex explanation. However, this couple refused to accept my straightforward and natural explanation of "misdiagnosis." It must have made them feel very important that their God would deign to clean out those carotid arteries in such a miraculous fashion.

Several months before the above carotid artery "miracle" report, I had participated in a public conference regarding whether or not miracles happen at all. The conference was sponsored by the local newspaper. One participant in the conference considered it a supernatural miracle that the World Trade Center towers' collapse didn't kill thousands more than the nearly 3,000 that were killed on September 11, 2001. WOW!

If almighty God were there on that awful day in New York performing a miracle, why in hell didn't he simply snuff out the fire? Or better yet, snuff out the lives of the Muslim hijackers before they flew into the towers? Or was Allah's power to perform a miracle more powerful than that of God or Yahweh when those thousands of Christians, Jews and non-believers perished so unjustly? If you ask these questions of the believer, you will likely receive some quite sincere answer like any of the following:

God works in mysterious ways; man is too sinful and ignorant to understand; scripture says God punishes the wicked; God allows man to freely mess up; man somehow did not do his part in God's plan; God's plan is one of infinite wisdom, we should not question it!

On an awful Saturday, February 1, 2003, the space shuttle Columbia and all its crew burned on re-entry and broke up over a thousand square miles of Texas. CNN quoted a witness saying "It was a miracle and only by the grace of God that no one was killed by the tons of falling debris."

Think of the simple math of the matter. That thousand square mile debris field was less than one-half of one percent of the area of Texas. And if the shuttle broke into an extreme number of 1,000,000 pieces, each separate piece would have over 27,000 square feet to land on. A miracle doesn't seem so necessary when you look at it realistically. Besides, if there had been a loving or powerful miracle worker around on that awful day, I could think of a better use of the miraculous power. The real "miracle" or wonder to me is how rational people can create supernatural miracles out of such clearly human and natural situations.

However, if you still insist on the possibility of real supernatural miracles, you may want to challenge the magician-turned-scientist, James Randi, who insists there are no such things as supernatural miracles. He puts a lot of his money where his mouth is. If you "know" of a real miracle, feel free to make an internet contact with the James Randi Educational Foundation to make your supernatural claim. You may collect more than a million dollars if you prove your claim. Over many decades the uncollected fortune has continued to grow as The Amazing Randi has never failed to duplicate or rationally explain any so-called miracle or supernatural phenomenon with which he has been challenged.

There is another respectable organization that examines miraculous claims for their validity. However, it offers no million dollar reward if its scientists fail to prove the totally natural character of the "miracle." The Council for Secular Humanism sponsors the Committee for Scientific Inquiry (CSI). If you have a miracle to be evaluated, feel free to contact this committee via the internet.

ANYTHING GOES IN THE NAME OF RELIGION?

You do not have to look long to find yet further extremes based on different religious beliefs. An ancient absurdity continues even today just seventy miles outside of Mexico City. Here men beat themselves bloody on Good Friday, commemorating the day when Christians believe Christ already died to pay for the sins of all. Some witnesses of the annual Mexican spectacle expressed disapproval of these bloody demonstrations. However, at least one tourist heartily approved as she said *"they are doing what they are doing out of faith."*

If I believe you are of a different color or race than the race chosen by my God, am I therefore allowed to consider you inferior? Hitler's Storm troopers' uniforms proclaimed "God With Us" while they helped exterminate millions of God's chosen people. If a believer re-writes history, burns a competitive church or synagogue, lies to children, confuses minds and tortures bodies "out of faith," do you suppose that excuses? Are such things acceptable merely because "they are doing what they are doing *out of faith*"? I don't think so.

CAN A POPULAR PRESIDENT LEAD US TO THEOCRACY?

President George W. Bush, by executive order, on January 29, 2001, established a special White House Office of Faith-based and Community Initiatives *in our White House!* This White House Office was set up to make it easier for religious organizations to apply for and receive direct governmental grants of public tax money. While this executive act may have been within the president's power or right, one might question the balanced wisdom of it.

Just over a year later, president George W. Bush, again within the scope of his executive power, led the United States in a National Day of Prayer on May 2, 2002. At the special White House ceremony making that day a National Day of Prayer, Mr. Bush said that *prayer* "strengthens our commitment to things that last and things that matter. It strengthens our love for one another." Would it have been more meaningful to have said exactly the same words about reason rather than prayer? Logical reason really does strengthen "our commitment to things that last and things that matter," like scientific knowledge that cures diseases, like intelligent planning that reduces warlike bloodshed, prevents job-losses, poverty and over-crowding. Right reason does deepen our love for one another, as it sees the respectful wisdom of The Golden Rule even in a pluralistic world.

If reason, rather than faith, ruled the George W. Bush administration, would the Moses-like choice to invade Iraq because of imaginary weapons of mass destruction have been made? Or is it more likely that reasonable alternatives would have been developed through more energetic negotiations? Praying for our troops and the thousands of dead and broken Iraqis on a National Day of Prayer might just appear hypocritical to most astute observers.

Aggravating this sort of missionary use of presidential time and effort was the fact that millions of office workers, firemen, and policemen nationwide also took a break from productive jobs to hear such a politically correct message and bow their heads in an attitude of public prayer. Would life in our pluralistic society run smoother if all Christians followed at least that one strong and clearly stated directive attributed to Christ (Matthew 6:5-6) when he commanded his followers to pray, not in public like the hypocrites, but in the secrecy of their rooms? At least, if they did their praying on their own time, they would waste less of the taxpayers' money.

This is the same President Bush who had named Jesus Christ his principal philosopher on the campaign trail. I agree with the insightful columnist, Helen Thomas (*Seattle Times,* 7/14/02, P. E2), that no others of our presidents have gone so far in their missionary zeal; rather, in keeping their spiritual views out of the public arena, they showed their understanding of their secular role.

A thoughtful person might well agree with Ms. Thomas when she further states that Mr. "Bush, in wrapping religious cloaks around the presidency, has a goal that is alien to what the Founders of our nation had in mind." I personally think that, though Mr. Bush has made jokes about his having graduated at the very bottom of his college class, it is becoming less and less a joking matter.

America became what she is today largely by preserving a common sense ability to ignore religious enthusiasts' extreme conclusions and demands. This has, to date, allowed a practical Jeffersonian Wall of Separation between Church and State in America. But if America continues to move toward Christian religious extremism, and if those with reasonable common sense continue to get increasingly drowned out by the powerful pulpits of the conservative Christians and their politicians, America could slide faster and faster toward theocracy. America's great stature in the world may well slip toward that of other theocracies, unless, of course, the general citizenry promptly starts voting in as great numbers as the conservative Christians do.

As I have gotten older, I observe more of the growing tyranny of the Christian majority in this great land of ours. Some of today's religious leaders seem quite willing to remove the essential bricks from the Jeffersonian wall separating Church and State even though the best constitutional scholars object. "CHURCH AND STATE—MUST INTEGRATE" has recently shown up as graffiti.

Such right-wingers would slow research as they declare a combination of two or four cells to be an actual human being even though the best scientists object. They would deny a free woman's right to choose whether to become or remain pregnant, with little if any consideration of the circumstances of that pregnancy. Their faith drives them to an arrogance that seems to ignore the rights of disagreeing individuals and minorities, no matter how thoughtful.

While this credulous arrogance repulses a lot of citizens, it is nevertheless being allowed to grow so rapidly that it could threaten our democratic, pluralistic American life. Freedoms can be stealthily taken away while those who are free do nothing. Freedom is not free, and we all need to exercise our voting rights more conscientiously, or the dire predictions of theocracy taking over from democracy may come true, yes, even in America.

We all have the same basic, *natural* needs and characteristics. Without supernatural matters of faith becoming involved, reasoning mankind does fairly well dealing with each other in the real world. This explains why our U.S. Constitution has preserved American democracy so long: while recorded believers still outnumber non-believers, most of both groups generally have abided by the Constitution, which successfully ignores the divisive differences of belief systems.

As you continue to wrestle with old beliefs bestowed in your pre-rational days, and as you try to find better ways to get along with the rest of mankind in your more mature days, realize that others are fighting or have fought similar battles. We all received our earliest and most impressive lessons in our pre-rational days when we were naturally and justifiably pretty credulous. Some of the many struggles between believers and non-believers continue because individuals (and societies) mature at different rates.

Neither individuals nor societies develop evenly and in lock-step fashion as they proceed from childhood dependency to adult self-sufficiency. This may explain why democracy is so messy and is the worst form of government in the world except for all the others. This ragged development can be seen to imitate or reflect the broader general development of the historic human society from the dark ages of faith to our more scientific age.

As shown through explorations of inner and outer space, mankind has made a lot of progress toward knowledge and self-confidence since Moses commanded his followers to stay away from the Tree of Knowledge. It is easier, therefore, for modern individuals to realize and enjoy their self-sufficiency than it was for individuals in past ages of belief. Yet the growth will likely remain jagged and fitful, because some today work hard to grow in new knowledge while others hold that it is terribly important to preserve old mysteries and traditions.

Some stay stuck in the past honestly while others who profit from traditional beliefs and superstitions may deliberately hold others from developing into independent thinkers for their own manipulative purposes, because of their own vested interests. The former who are honestly trying to help themselves and the rest of mankind to grow up deserve patient cooperation and tolerance; the latter, who would manipulatively impede man's progress toward self-sufficiency, deserve our harshest criticism. This latter group comes in for strong criticism, because they want to hold mankind down for selfish reasons. This group contains those insincere religious leaders who would like to have a theocratic type of government so that they can access more cheap power and more absolute control.

Recognize with legitimate alarm how the citizens of Provo, Utah, the most theocratic state in America, seem to tolerate the following situation. In that city, a sculpture called "Appeal to Divine Providence" shows the non-Christian founders of this country, Jefferson, John Adams and Ben Franklin kneeling in an apparent attitude of prayer while holding the Declaration of Independence. These men were far from praying Christians, but the false implication of that sculpture will, in its own subtle way, impede some young citizens of Provo indefinitely. Of course, it is easier for the credulous to believe than to study history! It is also easier to manipulate minds filled with imaginary mystery than those filled with factual history.

Democracy wherein thinking citizens govern themselves cannot long survive with theocracy wherein believing citizens allow themselves to be governed by representatives of God. Both history, especially history of the Middle East which cradled all the Abrahamic religions, and current events make this abundantly clear. Conversely, theocracy cannot control the citizens or long survive in a truly pluralistic democracy that does not tolerate the majority's tyranny over minorities. One can only guess at how vastly the growing pains of Afghanistan and Iraq would diminish if their potential leaders could accept the above fact.

Nevertheless, as the American right wing continues to attack our Jeffersonian Wall of Separation of Church and State, I wonder how long it will take to demolish that important wall. We already have a president with an Office of Religion in our White House; he has declared a National Prayer Day and seems to make more effort to live by the Bible than the Constitution. In many public ways he appears to be more a zealous Christian missionary than a secular leader in a pluralistic world.

We are well beyond the beginning stages of demolition of the Jeffersonian Wall of Separation. More than just the camel's nose has already snuck into the inclusive tent of democracy. If neglected, this powerful camel could ruin the whole tent. And if you think that is an extreme statement, please analyze the basic causes of most of the modern wars in societies much older than our own.

CHRISTIANS CLAIM AMERICA AS THEIR OWN

I am a patriotic citizen of the United States and the World, but especially of the United States. Yet I receive often-repeated e-mails insisting that if I don't like America being Christian, just leave. Also, if I don't like the slogan "In God We Trust" as our national motto, then according to these Christians, I should just go elsewhere.

Newsflash! Contrary to these anti-historical e-mails, this nation was not founded on Christian principles. I really do think the great Thomas Jefferson and John Adams rank as two of our country's most outstanding founding fathers. William Edelen (*Toward the Mystery*, Joslyn & Morris, Inc., pp. 88-89) assembled a few of the obviously non-Christian thoughts from these founders.

Jefferson held that "Christianity had become the most perverted system that ever shone on man" and that "the teachings of Jesus have come to us mutilated, misstated and unintelligible." This is the same Jefferson who wrote to John Adams: "The day will come when the mystical generation of Jesus by the supreme being as his father in the womb of a virgin will be classed with the fable of the generation of Minerva in the brain of Jupiter."

And John Adams wrote to Thomas Jefferson, "Tom, had you and I been 40 days with Moses and beheld the great God, and even if God himself had tried to tell us that three was one... and one equals three, you and I would never have believed it. We would never fall victims to such lies." **These most influential founders were not Christian!** And I would hope that those denying history by insisting otherwise could be ignored to the extent that they would not be allowed to re-write history.

The 1776 Declaration of Independence from a religious and tyrannical King George III, "by the grace of God, King of England and head of its church," mentions God twice. However, by 1787 (a mere eleven years later) in the more mature and detailed United States Constitution, there is no reference to a God at all. It simply does not propound theism, agnosticism, atheism, or any kind of sectarianism. It is surely no accident that it is the longest lasting federal constitution in existence. (It is noteworthy that in June 2003 the drafters of the new European Union Constitution likewise finalized that important twenty-first century document without any reference to a God or Christianity.)

Sincere, enthusiastic faith unfettered by reason, can motivate unforeseeable extremes and challenges to reason. John Adams, James Madison and Thomas Jefferson recognized clearly that the stable State must securely stay free from religious matters or belief systems and opinions that can so readily divide humankind. That is why Thomas Jefferson saw the Wall of Separation as so important; and that is why it is so important that the United States maintain the honest, reasoned and disciplined observance of our Constitution.

The above list of faith-based extremes could be much longer. I am confident you have observed other examples of people unwilling or unable to grow free of the past. Growth can be challenging especially when it involves growth to independence of an addiction.

In the first half of the twentieth century, the majority of American citizens did not see smoking as absurd. But now smoking by adults in the twenty-first century is quite generally accepted as absurd. Yet tobacco, the obvious carcinogen, remains popular with some addicted and wish-fulfilling victims today though they now know intellectually that it is commonly harmful to use it.

Is it possible that religion with its supernatural mysteries and divine comforts has become for some believers what nicotine is to the die-hard smoker? The majority of U.S. citizens learned that smoking was absurd well before the end of the twentieth century; yet millions of wish fulfilling smokers remain enslaved to nicotine over a generation later. It seems fair to wonder how long a similar dynamic of addictive wish fulfillment will preserve old superstitions that sometimes lead to unreasonable extremes even after entering the age of reason.

SEQUITUR/NON SEQUITUR—BELIEF IN GENIES

A husband takes his wife to play her first game of golf. The wife promptly hacked her first shot right through the window of the biggest house adjacent to the course. The husband cringed, "I warned you to be careful!" Now we'll have to go up there, find the owner, apologize and see how much your lousy drive is going to cost us."

So the couple walked up to the house and knocked on the door. A warm voice said, "Come on in." When they opened the door they saw the damage that was done: glass was all over the place, and a broken antique bottle was lying on its side near the broken window. A man reclining on the couch asked, "Are you the people that broke my window?" "Uh…yeah, sir. We're sure sorry about that," the husband replied. "Oh, no apology is necessary. Actually I want to thank you. You see, I'm a genie, and I've been trapped in that bottle for a thousand years. Now that you've released me,

I'm allowed to grant three wishes. I'll give you each one wish, but if you don't mind, I'll keep the last one for myself." "Wow, that's great!" the husband said. He pondered a moment and blurted out, "I'd like a million dollars a year for the rest of my life." "No problem," said the genie. "You've got it, it's the least I can do. And I'll guarantee you a long, healthy life!" And now you, young lady, what do you want?" the genie asked. "I'd like to own a gorgeous home complete with servants in every country in the world," she said. "Consider it done," the genie said. "And your homes will always be safe from fire, burglary and natural disasters!"

"And now," the couple asked in unison, "what's your wish, genie?" "Well, since I've been trapped in that bottle and haven't been with a woman in more than a thousand years, my wish is to have sex with your wife." The husband looked at his wife and said, "Gee, honey, you know we both now have a fortune, and all those houses. What do you think?" She mulled it over for a few moments and said, "You know, you're right. Considering our good fortune. I guess I wouldn't mind, but what about you, honey?" "You know I love you, sweetheart," said the husband. "I'd do the same for you!"

So the genie and the woman went upstairs where they spent the rest of the afternoon enjoying each other. The genie was insatiable. After about three hours of non-stop sex, the genie rolled over and looked directly into her eyes and asked, "How old are you and your husband?" "Why we're both thirty-five," she responded breathlessly. " No shit. Thirty–five years old and both of you still believe in genies?"

SEVEN

HUMILITY IS TRUTH—
TRUTH IS HUMILITY

You may call me a proud sinner, but I try to go where the facts of history and my intellect lead me in the twenty-first century. I challenge old ways that have become counterproductive. The Dark Ages seem to me outdated. Now may be the time to re-examine the traditional vestiges of those credulous times as we see more of the harm that old superstitions can cause. Human beings have evolved into very complex thinking animals; it would be the greatest insult to nature to become less the thinker and more the believer of old. I think nature put our eyes in front so that we can go forward rather than backward; however, some more conservative individuals might try to make a case somehow that our eyes are actually in back of our head and we are designed to preserve the past.

I think we modern humans, to be humbly true to ourselves, ought to question whether we are to remain bound by past ignorance and superstitions that historically divided and impeded humankind. With improving education and technology, human knowledge continues to double at an ever-increasing rate. To live and act according to the prejudices, assumptions and superstitions that divided our ancestors in darker times would be a great immorality; it would be the practical denial of our own inner, highest power, our reason or intellect.

A stark example of putting faith ahead of reason appeared in the news June 15, 2002. Rev. Jacques Robidoux, leader of a Massachusetts religious sect, followed "instructions from God" and watched his ten-month-old son literally starve to death. The reverend father of the child believed that his sister had received a vision from God telling the parents to stop all feeding of solid food. The twenty-first century jury did not like this obvious insult to nature; they realized that visions and dreams are not reliable guides for behavior. Robidoux was convicted of first-degree murder; his wife, the child's biological mother, was charged with second degree murder.

Humble believers understand that true humility is reality-based. Humility is not lowliness except for the lowly. For the intelligent, rational human being who is true to his great humanity, humility is a truthful, high-minded acceptance of how awesome it is to be human. Think! Think, and be true to yourself, be proud of your spiritual or mental ability to think and know. Rejoice at progress; be not afraid to go forward as you use the discoveries of science in this new century and continue to "eat of the Tree of Knowledge."

That ability to know, to remember, to think, to cooperate with our fellows and thereby develop solutions to very complex problems, sets us apart from the other animals; it also helps us go where our forefathers could hardly dream of going. A human can't run as fast as a cheetah, is not as strong as an elephant, cannot see as clearly as the eagle. Yet a rational human being is far superior to all the other animals, because he has the potential to think, to record history, to learn from the past, to make tools, and to cooperate with others who have also learned from the past. Because of thoughtful cooperation and the ability to learn from the past, humans can now move much faster than the cheetah, can move greater loads than the elephant and see much farther than the eagle.

This is fact, this is the truth about human nature—our ability to think is what makes us able to be great. If we think, we can be great; if we quit thinking clearly, we stop progressing toward our greatness. And twenty-first century citizens can think and know much better than could our ancestors. Much thanks to those ancestors, especially those who were independent thinkers like Galileo, Copernicus, Newton, Jefferson, Paine, Einstein and Watson.

A person can be great; he does not have to be great. One can think; one does not have to think. Thomas Aquinas defined man as *animal rationalis* (a rational animal); I think he should have added a third word: *animal potentialiter rationalis* (a potentially rational animal). A person can remain as a child, fail to develop his potential to think logically and clearly. A person can passively avoid the Tree of Knowledge and remain ignorant of the facts of modern life! Or a person can choose to work, study, learn and develop his ability to think as a rational person using modern tools of growth.

The lowly or intellectually lazy person is easy prey for the false prophets looking for profits and power wherever they can be found. The wishful thinkers appear to be intellectually lazy and lowly persons who find it easy to fall for all kinds of promising pitches for opiates of mind and body. These suggestible people buy drugs and superstitions, because they want to believe, like dependent children, that help will somehow come from outside or from above.

My own observation is that there is no magic, superstition or miraculous scheme that really works as it claims to defy the natural laws of causality. We have to actively grasp and use our modern tools if we are to contribute to personal or societal progress. Wishing is not very effective by itself; it takes work, sometimes hard work, to rise above the past. This brings to mind the following brief newspaper want ad: "For Sale—Nordic track exerciser, $300—hardly used. Call Chubby." Get real, Chubby; quit wishing and start sweating!

We owe it to ourselves, as caring citizens, to be alert lest we become too trusting, too credulous, too customary. We need to be on our guard lest we trust too easily without verifying the statements and stances of public figures, no matter how they are dressed or how powerful their megaphone. It is only reasonable that we challenge and verify the public positions of popular preachers and politicians when they use half-truths or superstitions to gain power and influence over the unwary. Eternal vigilance is the price of freedom.

POLITICIANS READILY JOIN THE BELIEVERS

When the judge asked Willie Sutton why he robbed banks, the thief answered, "Because that's where the money is." Is this why politicians find it so hard to resist churches? That's where the believers are! Politicians know that if they can at least appear religious, they will attract easy listeners. Preachers, too, recognize the resulting cheap power they can exert on the political process. The result is too often one of mutually addictive dependency: politicians depending on preachers and preachers depending on politicians. It behooves us moderns to recognize that the union of Cross and Crown has already been tried and found wanting.

Rather than allowing unmerited power to become centered in the pulpits of the non-elected, thinking citizens must help the superhuman to achieve realistic humility. I do not mean lowliness. Many of these talented preachers could become good counselors and social workers if they just dropped one gratuitous assumption. Humility is not lowliness; humility is truth. Therefore thinking men need to find practical ways to help these preachers get down from their supernaturally high horses so that they can become productive as mere thinking human beings.

The basic assumption that God elevates and enlightens special representatives to bestow supernatural wisdom on the masses of rational humanity fails to stand up to the light of clear reason. During the darker ages when the shamans and the clergy were better educated than the rest of society, authority-based superstitions were tried and found wanting. By way of contrast, observe that since the Dark Ages, with more and more scientists energetically climbing the tree of human knowledge, the resulting productivity of the masses has multiplied impressively. Instead of cowering before the tree of scientific knowledge as scared little children, we embrace it. Now we recognize our ability to communicate and democratically govern ourselves responsibly.

If Moses had been humble enough, realistic enough, to recognize his limitations, he might have surrounded himself with effective lieutenants who could have helped him think through the common challenges of disciplining the masses. Together they may have kept the people from eating spoiled pork and taking part in self-destructive heathen parties. Surely they would have been more cooperative and less genocidal with the "heathens" as the Hebrews wandered through those heathens' territories.

But, no, not megalomanic Moses! He had the ear of his almighty God, a jealous God, an angry and demanding God. If Moses had humbly admitted his need for real help and shown himself capable of leading leaders, I doubt that his people would have needed forty years to get from Egypt to their promised land. After all, this land of promise was not very far away; from present-day Cairo to Jerusalem is only 265 miles. But Moses relied on Moses and his dictatorial commandments, so he did not adequately delegate power to strong, thinking lieutenants, nor did he cooperate adequately with knowledgeable heathen neighbors.

Moses chose to elevate his followers to a divinely chosen super race ruled by a superhuman leader. "We are better than the neighbors and must not mix with them; we must not contaminate ourselves with these heathens and their evil ways. Listen to me, obey me, and I will show you a land flowing with milk and honey." Yeah, right there in the Middle Eastern desert.

The majority of Jews held on to the fear of Yahweh so strongly that vestiges of that old fear remain in the twenty-first century. As *Fiddler on the Roof* made beautifully clear, Jewish traditions die hard, very hard! Just as the assumption of God's existence and power kept this race meandering and fighting in the deserts of the Middle East for many decades, the continued assumption of a Yahweh and Allah today impedes Israel and her Palestinian brothers from ready rational compromises regarding freedom of movement, wailing-wall spaces and other shrines of old so-called holy places.

Moses' megalomanic approach to leadership also worked for Christian kings and queens who used their assumed divine rights to pursue empires while spreading the gospels of guilt and grace throughout the western world. And, yes, it appeared that God showed his divine pleasure as "blessed" kings, queens and popes conquered the best lands known to man! *"In hoc signo vinces!"* "In this sign you will conquer!" is the message Constantine is said to have seen or dreamed he saw in the sky along with a cross. You see, dreams, visions and prophecies based thereon can change the world.

Obviously Moses wasn't the only one who saw supernatural visions to get extra killing power and easy votes. Even Hitler's soldiers had "God with us" *(Gott mitt ums)* on their uniform belt buckles as they tried to conquer the lesser races. All of these leaders took the uncompromising position that We Are Right, and over and over again that spelled W.A.R.

If the destructiveness of this sort of megalomania were only a problem of old, we could laugh at it and go on. But, sad to say, we still have leaders at home and abroad who want the cheap power that assumed divinity can provide in order to get or keep control of the credulous. A *New York Times* editorial (2/12/06) pointed out that Bush is the president who has most often asked us to "...just trust him. We... can't think of a president who has that trust less." Evidently the *New York Times* is not alone in this conviction. If you had *Googled* the phrase "George W. Bush lies" on 2/12/06, you would have found over 369,000 references. By 2/12/09, a mere three years later, this large figure had grown to a huge 49,100,000 references. Humility is truth, and this holds for this most religious president as for the rest of us.

POLITICIANS NEED TO KNOW WE CAN THINK

Grasping for cheap power, made much easier by the God assumption, has gone on for millennia. It will likely continue until we as a human race have the courage, the self-respect, the self-esteem to say "Hold, enough!" We do not need to believe blindly in fairy tales, superstitions or gratuitous assumptions any more. We humbly, truthfully respect the rational human mind enough to use it to learn more of this wonderful world and follow where those facts lead. This good mind urges us to improve and help others to enjoy the freedom to improve themselves also. Growth, forward-looking progress, is natural; it is good.

I fondly hope that each and every one of us can soon come to relax and enjoy admitting to ourselves that we are most truly human when we think and act responsibly. We want to follow The Golden Rule, by which we treat others as we would reasonably want and expect them to treat us if our roles were reversed. We want all to live rational lives so that everyone demonstrates respect for self and others by working to make this one and only knowable life the reasonable best it can be. We think that if we hurt a fellow human being, we do not need to confess to or apologize to some God; we do need to try to help that human being get back on his road to happiness. This is being true to our humanity, the humanity shared with the person we may have hurt. This is true humility, the source of healthy human pride—a pride that rejoices not only in one's own achievements but also in the responsible achievements of our other human neighbors on this small planet.

SEQUITUR/NON SEQUITUR—
INTENTIONS VERSUS REALITY

Old Fred's hospital bed was surrounded by well-wishers; it didn't look good for Fred. Suddenly he motioned to the pastor for something to write on. The pastor lovingly handed him a pen and paper. Fred used his last bit of energy to scribble a note, turned blue and died. The pastor thought it best not to look at the note right there, so he placed it in his jacket pocket.

At Fred's funeral, as the pastor was finishing his eulogy, he realized he was wearing the same jacket he wore when Fred died.

"Fred handed me a note just before he died," he said. "I have not looked at it, but knowing Fred, I am sure there's a word of inspiration in it for all of us."

Opening the note, he read aloud, "Help! You're standing on my oxygen tube!"

EIGHT

PRACTICAL ATHEISM

Congratulations are in order if you have thoughtfully progressed this far with me. Surely we have lost many fellow travelers; we may have run too fast for them. We have often taken closely argued positions that may be so new and untraditional that they are not readily comfortable. We progress at different rates. Our positions have frequently undermined traditions and threatened deeply ensconced vested interests, in high places and low. Congratulations if you are now more able to appreciate how an unwarranted assumption of the unseen, unknown and unknowable, can impede our human progress.

Today we cannot take any responsibility for the ancient telling of tall tales, myths, mistakes and ignorance of past generations; but in this information age we need not continue to be victims of such blindness either. What Moses and St. Thomas freely, gratuitously, assumed and asserted, we can freely deny. This demonstrates an accepted principle of logic and law: anything that is gratuitously asserted can be gratuitously denied.

Many molders of public opinion today have held on to the old assumption of a God who, they say, deserves respect and obedience. Instead of listening to these messengers of an assumed world, we may be better served by the wisdom of Mark Twain. He humbly admitted that "it ain't what I don't know that gets me in trouble; it's what I know for sure that ain't so—that's what gets me in trouble."

By now you can likely appreciate the practical need for frank and truthful humility regarding the old improbable assumption of the existence of some perfect and loving God. We have seen over and over how supernatural faith has been involved when the human race gets itself into its most difficult scrapes—from Ahuramazda to Zeus, not one God of the total pantheon has actually lifted a finger to lighten our natural load of human responsibilities.

Look around you and observe all the world's evils and imperfections, the tsunamis, the hurricanes, floods, droughts, religious absurdities, childhood cancers, and other diseases. Look at the natural economy of the big fish eating the little fish, the powerful fox crushing the weaker rabbit, the pain and suffering in nature's economy of the survival of the fittest. Surely it makes you wonder how these could possibly be evidence of a supposed powerful, wise and loving God. Such evident divine impotence or lack of love gives us strong arguments against there being a perfect God at all. And one of the very strongest arguments for there being no God at all is given by the most enthusiastic believers themselves. In the name of their Gods, *jihads* of all sorts have divided and killed millions for centuries, in crusade after crusade (biblical, modern and in between).

The headline "Faithful religionists attack atheists and other heretics" would hardly raise an eyebrow. By contrast, have you *ever* seen a headline like "Agnostics killing humanists to convert them"? Or "Angry atheists attack agnostics and skeptics for their heresies"? It is unlikely you ever will. "By their fruits you shall know them" is supposed to have come straight from the lips of Christ. Can you get bad fruit from a good tree? Humankind is still harvesting a lot of bad fruit from the trees of the God assumption and the thousands of divisive cults and sects springing from that assumption. And these divisive sects keep multiplying their schisms in the twenty-first century as they splinter further into those religious groups who, for example, reject homosexuals versus those that accept homosexuals as good human beings.

PRAGMATISM TO THE RESCUE?

It is futile for natural man to try to logically prove or disprove an assumed supernatural being; it is simply beyond man's ability to know beyond this world of nature. (Try lifting yourself by your own ankles. Or directly study your own brain in a state of total inactivity.) Logically we must humbly admit that we don't know, we can't know with purely logical certainty of any supernatural being. As purely natural human beings, we can only know of this natural universe. Of course, as imaginative beings, not constrained by reason, we can imagine or assume anything, real or not; in our imaginations, hopes and dreams, we can create anything, but that does not make any of it objectively real.

However, pragmatically or practically speaking, the natural evidence of no supernatural caring power can be quite convincing. The ancient Greek philosopher, Epicurus (ca. 300 B.P.E.), made this very brief but strong case for No Good God: "Is God willing to prevent evil, but not able? Then he is not omnipotent. Is he able, but not willing? Then he is malevolent. Is he both able and willing? Then whence cometh evil? Is he neither able nor willing? Then why call him God?" These are important questions that beg for thoughtful answers. Try asking these Epicurean questions in situations such as: tsunamis, earthquakes and hurricanes destroying innocent families and homes, floods, droughts, wars, famines, epidemics, holocausts and other genocides.

Once we collectively have the truthful humility to admit

that we are just natural, rational human beings who do not owe anything to Anyone outside this great natural world, we will be able to shed a myriad of impediments to progress in our challenging battles with nature. Epicurus now makes so much sense that I think those fellow human beings who insist that they have supernatural knowledge may reasonably be seen to be victims of their own imaginations or of incorrigible pride. But, remember, if they are sincere, not hypocritical nor manipulative, conscientious, true to themselves, it behooves us to be tolerant and accepting of them as neighbors on this small planet! Everyone progresses at his own rate.

FEAR AND GREED UNDER CONTROL

You have already seen how powerful and controlling fear of hell and greed for grace and heaven can be for many. However, if man is to be free, he must be in control, not a slave to fear or greed, not addicted to anything. But how can he overcome the attractive addiction to such fear and greed?

If the Old Testament Jews had told Moses he may have been overcome by desert heat when he saw his burning bush, they would not have given him such inordinate power over them. It is reasonable to suppose that Moses did hallucinate in the heat and hunger of his long and lonely fast in the desert. After all, he had isolated himself from his fellows for an extreme amount of time, apparently without food or much drink for all that time. This is nearly perfect psychological preparation for hallucinations and loss of reality contact.

Isn't it interesting that all three of the world's greatest organized religions originated in the Middle East? None of the three founders, Moses, Jesus, or Muhammad, came from a stabilizing or standard family background. Judaism, Christianity and Islamism all had articulate and street-smart founders without ordinary father figures in their young lives, and all three had fasted and isolated themselves from others in the desert heat for extended periods. Then these founders communicated with their followers with assumed divine strength and superior wisdom. Was their God a wish-fulfilling assumption based on imaginary hallucinations or, perhaps, the megalomanic need for cheap power to manipulate their followers?

Moses could threaten the Jews of old with the anger and jealousy of a God hurling thunderbolts. Modern men listen to meteorologists explain the weather, so they do not assume nor fear a God of the Storm as in King David's time. Knowledge of static electricity surely does not diminish our awe of a great lightning show. But such a powerful show does not cause us to assume there is a divine hurler of thunderbolts trying to scare us into submission. Such ignorance-based fear may have worked for Moses and David; with the growth of scientific knowledge, it is no longer appropriate nor popular. Modern man has eaten of the Tree of Knowledge (science), continues to do so at a quickening pace, and that is good!

What would actually change in your real world if you no longer assumed a power greater than nature? What if all of us refused to cower in fear and confidently took the responsibility to think things through on our own? What would happen if we assumed there is no divine power? Of course, the religious terrorists would try to make sure there was a lot of hell to pay for such an assumption. As part of John Lennon's efforts to unify mankind he invited us to "*Imagine* there's no heaven," and he was hounded by the F.B.I. Even here in the twenty-first century, such an assumption of no supernatural power still causes a great gnashing of self-righteous teeth in those who think everyone should be dependent on some power higher than a well-functioning human mind.

An example of this self-righteous gnashing of teeth at a non-believer: Before 2004, David Habecker had been elected four times to the town Board of Estes Park, Colorado. After he had served almost thirteen years as town trustee, it happened that, without a Board vote, the mayor agreed with another trustee's suggestion that the Pledge of Allegiance be recited before Board meetings. So when Mr. Habecker refused to stand during the religious Pledge of Allegiance "under God," a recall petition was begun. And even in the "enlightened" town of Estes Park, Colorado, he was recalled by a vote of 903 to 605.

If the gratuitous God assumption were not accepted, the kings of the powerful pulpits would lose their divine rights, their cheap power, since they could no longer effectively claim to be "by the grace of God, king." Insurance companies could not escape their responsibilities by using the phrase "except for acts of God." Phony snake oil and drug salesmen selling miraculously cheap power to the greedy, ignorant, lazy or insecure, would have to get real jobs based on human abilities and skills. Those running dependency engendering twelve-step programs to shift personal responsibility to a Higher Power would have to abandon such cheap power plays and really study to understand the addictive personality. Careful, the sky might fall!

PROGRESS TOWARD RATIONALISM

Down through the centuries, humankind has progressed through many forms of polytheism. Bad Gods and good Gods of love, war, the hunt, storms, light, darkness, rain, good, evil, etc. were assumed into existence from myths of old. Imaginative syncretism synthesized these Gods from the great rumor mills of history as well as pre-history. Man has always wanted to have more and to know more than he is quite able to accomplish alone. So pre-scientific man created Gods of all sorts, made idols of those Gods and sold them by the carloads (for *real* profits)—and the beat continues among some lesser tribes. For most people, though, as man has developed better ways to hunt and feed himself, there is no more need for a God of the hunt. With modern meteorology, we do not need a rain God; and with astronomy we do not need the superstitions of astrology.

As man pursues and achieves ever fuller knowledge of nature, no superstitious assumption is needed to fill the human stomach and heart. The modern scientific farmer, with his hybrid seeds and irrigation skills, now harvests over two hundred bushels of corn per acre from the same land where his grandfather may have harvested less than forty bushels. Scientific understanding of facts, not unfounded assumptions, is the best source of fulfillment and excitement for the human spirit.

With the spread of education, polytheism has mostly disappeared. Yes, some still hang on to a God of good and a God of evil (Satan); others hang on to the concept of angels as lesser gods or messengers for God. Most believers, though, hold that if God is almighty, he does not need helpers to get the word out (except, of course, for the self-appointed missionaries and manipulators to take up the collections of guilt-offerings). Some romantics like to hang onto the concept of angels existing; they are so warm, cuddly and comforting in such a cold and insecure world. Besides, they sell well in gift shops (right alongside the teddy bears).

WILL MONOTHEISM DISAPPEAR WITH POLYTHEISM?

For all practical purposes, most Gods have been dropped from man's repertoire of mythical creations. Sure, every week we still have Wednesday (Woden's day) followed by Thor's Day, but does anyone still believe these old Gods have any power? I know of no Wodenists today; everyone is an aWodenist these days. So, too, everyone I know is an aThorist; none of my acquaintances believe in Thor anymore. Likewise, most people are atheists as regards all Gods but the one at the top for them. They are nontheists (atheists) regarding all of mankind's Gods but their own very favorite; they could be called mostly atheists or atheists plus or minus one. This theological progress has been painfully slow, while amazing human progress in natural knowledge continues at an ever-increasing pace. Actually there are huge numbers of philosphical agnostics and practical atheists out there. Now it is reasonable to wonder when humankind will be able to take the big step to independence and no longer assume even one God. The persons taking this final step could be called complete atheists.

Can modern, educated man become so self-responsible, so free from fear and greed that he can quit assuming a Higher Power, a power that was assumed to be almighty and loving but would not or could not stop the murderous faith-based twin tower attack of September 11, 2001? Considering the horrible pain and losses of nearly 3,000 families in that God-based attack, is it now time to re-evaluate the old assumption that a loving God, a Higher Power, exists, cares and is looking out for us? Was there really some God in charge of nature when a quarter of a million people perished in the great 2004 tsunami? Was there a God punishing New Orleans in 2005 when hurricane Katrina nearly drowned the city? Would it be more reasonable to assume that such a caring Higher Power simply does not exist? With Epicurus, we can ask, "If he could not or would not do anything about such 'evil,' why call him God?"

Why should educated man fear or love such an ineffective power? Or was it that the Allah of fear and guilt was more potent than the God of love on that awful morning of 9/11/01? If so, then where was the Allah of fear and guilt when so many thousands of Muslims perished in the 2004 tsunami? Educated man does not need to fear God, just those who overly enthusiastically believe in him. Bin Laden's God is not worthy of fear, but his enthusiastic, believing, zealous minions are. The God of the self-styled Army of God in America is not worthy of fear, but the enthusiastic, credulous minions of that Army are. Both groups, driven to their self-righteous extremes by their blinding faith in God, hold their truths to be self-evident, that as representatives of God they are above man's responsible laws; they apparently believe they are being virtuous in trying to destroy God's thinking enemies along with the Godless United States Constitution.

That thoughtful Godless Constitution protects the right of both God-assumers and pragmatic thinkers to attack each other's assumptions, opinions, and statements. Yet, for political and superstitious reasons, the following thought-provoking article could not make it into print at the end of the twentieth century. This essay very eloquently captures the point of the current chapter. I include it here **verbatim** with deep thanks to its author, James A. Haught, editor of *The Charleston (WV) Gazette*. Dr. Haught wrote:

"This essay was rejected by almost every mainstream U.S. magazine. In a nation of believers, it's extremely difficult to express skepticism in mainstream media. (I couldn't print it in my own newspaper.)"

LET'S OUTGROW FAIRY TALES

By James A. Haught

The supernatural spectrum is immense: Gods, goddesses, devils, demons, angels, heavens, hells, purgatories, limbos, miracles, prophecies, visions, auras, saviors, saints, virgin births, immaculate conceptions, resurrections, bodily ascensions, faith-healings, salvation, redemption, messages from the dead, voices from Atlantis, omens, clairvoyance, spirit-signals, spirit-possession, exorcisms, divine visitations, incarnations, reincarnations, second comings, judgment days, astrology horoscopes, psychic phenomena, psychic surgery, extra-sensory perception, telekinesis, second sight, voodoo, fairies, leprechauns, werewolves, vampires, zombies, witches, warlocks, ghosts, wraiths, poltergeists, dopplegangers, incubi, succubi, palmistry, tarot cards, ouija boards, levitation, out-of-body travel, magical transport to UFOs, Elvis on a flying saucer, invisible Lemurians in Mount Shasta, Thetans from a dying planet, etc., etc., etc.

All these magical beliefs have a common denominator: They lack tangible evidence. You can't test supernatural claims; you're supposed to accept them by blind faith. Their only backup is that they were "revealed by a prophet, guru, astrologer, shaman, mullah, mystic, swami, psychic, soothsayer or "channeler."

That's sufficient proof for billions of people. Most of humanity prays to invisible spirits and envisions mystical realms. Most politicians invoke the deities. Supernaturalism pervades our species, consuming billions of person-hours and trillions of dollars. Millions of prayers to unseen beings are uttered every hour, and millions of rituals performed. This extravaganza requires a vast array of priests and facilities. The cost is astronomical. Americans give $70 billion a year to churches and broadcast ministries—more than the national budgets of many countries. Other investment is enormous: Americans spend $300 million a year on psychic hotlines. Angel books and end-of-the-world books sell by millions.

Amid this global mishmash, I want to offer a lonely minority view: I think it's all fairy tales. Every last shred of it. The whole mystical array, from Jehovah and Beelzebub to Ramthis and the Lemurians, lacks any type of proof—unless you count weeping statues. My hunch is that every invisible spirit is imaginary. Therefore, the planet-spanning worship is expended on nothing.

I think that most intelligent, educated, scientific-minded people suspect that the spirit world doesn't exist. But they stay silent, because it's rude to question people's faith. However, what about honesty? Aren't conscientious thinkers obliged to speak the truth as they see it? Aren't logical people allowed to ask for evidence?

Some researchers recently concluded that the human species is "wired" for faith, that our DNA includes coding for mystery. Maybe—but what about exceptions like me and similar doubters? Why doesn't our wiring cause us to swallow the supernatural?

Moreover, even ardent believers see absurdity in rival religions. Consider these examples:

Millions of Hindus pray over statues of Shiva's phallus. Ask Presbyterians if they think there's an unseen Shiva who wants his anatomy utilized in worship.

Catholics say that the Virgin Mary makes periodic appearances to the faithful. Ask Muslims if it's true.

Mormons say that Jesus was transported to America after his resurrection. Ask Buddhists if they believe it—or if they even accept the resurrection.

Jehovah's Witnesses say that, any day now, Satan will come out of the earth with an army of demons, and Jesus will come out of the sky with an army of angels, and the Battle of Armageddon will kill everyone except Jehovah's Witnesses. Ask Jews if this is correct.

Florida's Santeria worshippers sacrifice dogs, goats, chickens and the like, tossing their bodies into waterways. Ask Baptists if the Santeria gods want animals to be killed.

Unification Church members say that Jesus visited master moon and told him to convert all people as "Moonies." Ask Methodists if this really occurred.

Muslim suicide bombers who sacrifice themselves in Israel are taught that martyrs go instantly to a paradise full of lovely female houri nymphs. Ask Lutherans if past bombers are now in heaven with houris.

Millions of American Pentecostals say that the Holy Ghost causes them to spout "the unknown tongue," a spontaneous outpouring of sounds. Ask Episcopalians if the third member of the Trinity causes this phenomenon.

Scientologists say that every human has a soul which is a "thetan" that came from another planet. Ask Seventh-day Adventists if this is true.

Aztecs sacrificed thousands of victims—cutting out hearts, killing children, skinning maidens—for various gods such as an invisible feathered serpent. Ask any current church if the invisible feathered serpent really existed.

During the witch hunts, inquisitor priests tortured thousands of women into confessing that they flew through the sky, changed into animals, blighted crops, copulated with Satan, etc. Ask any current church if the execution of "witches" was based on reality.

You see, most believers realize that other religions are bogus. Why do they think their own theology is different? I'm calling for the final step to honesty. If some magical spirits obviously are imaginary, it's logical to assume that others are similar.

The western world is turning more rational, more scientific. Education is dispelling superstition. Most advanced nations in Europe are abandoning belief in gods, devils, heavens, hells. Church attendance there has dwindled to a tiny fringe. America remains a bulwark of churchgoing—but educated Americans don't really expect divine intervention. If their children get pneumonia, they trust penicillin over prayer.

As for the familiar contention that supernatural beliefs make people more moral and humane, do you really think that Pat Robertson and Jerry Falwell are ethically superior to non-religious Americans?

Polls find that the more education people have, the fewer their religious convictions. Therefore, the educated are the natural group to break away from magic. I'd like to see a revolt by the intelligent against myths.

Generally, the educated class laughs at quacko miracle reports, but not at the prevailing majority religion. However, there's no logical reason to consider one supernatural claim superior to another. No matter how much it's cloaked in poetry and allegory, religion consists of worshipping spooks—imaginary ones, in my view.

The time has come for thinking Americans to say, publicly and bluntly: There's no reliable evidence of invisible spirits. Worshiping them is a waste of time and money. Instead, let's use our minds to improve life for people here and now. Fairy tales came from the primitive past, and they have no place in the 21st century.

(Note: *Repeated thanks to Dr. James A. Haught for providing the above summary essay.*)

NINE

LIFE WITHOUT GOD IN THE UNITED STATES

When I left the Catholic priesthood at the age of thirty-six, my youngest brother, then twenty-five, asked me seriously: "How can you be a moral man without God and the Church?" The answer was and is still very simply the same as it has been for the past forty years: "I live reasonably, true to my rational self; and there is no more reasonable means to good morality than The Golden Rule; this was well established long before the birth of Christianity."

I am not going to preach to you just how to apply The Golden Rule of treating others as you would reasonably want and expect to be treated if your roles were reversed. What I would rather do now is to picture some of what life in these United States could become if most of you were able to quit assuming there is a God or Higher Power. The great physicist, Isaac Newton, reputedly said "If I have been able to see further than others, it is because I have stood on the shoulders of giants." If you can reasonably balance yourselves on the best, tallest, and strongest shoulders of your giant ancestors, you will enjoy the view.

Consider standing tall on the shoulders of James Madison, John Adams, Thomas Jefferson, Ben Franklin, Albert Einstein, Mark Twain, Thomas Edison, Bertrand Russell, Robert Ingersol, Charles Darwin, Isaac Asimov, Isaac Newton, Nicolaus Copernicus, Carl Sagan, Ayn Rand and others like these skeptics, agnostics and atheists. Can you refuse to be bowed down under imagined guilt from an imagined Eden or crushed beneath the cross of a Roman Criminal? As you now stand on the shoulders of the above giants, can you now see humankind's progress from polytheism to monotheism and finally to a pragmatic and reasonable atheism? If you can see that far, you can also see a host of near-utopian improvements, improvements that to some will seem highly immoral (uncustomary).

As you look to the reasonable future, it will be helpful to understand more of the basic meaning of morality, what is basically involved in being moral or immoral. The word morality itself comes from the old Latin word *mos* (custom), *moris* (of custom). For example, the Latin phrase "*res moris*" simply means "a matter of custom." So the phrase "customary morality" is a tautology, self-repetitive. Similarly, the Greek word *ethos* (custom) gives us our word "ethics"; and again the phrase "customary ethics" is a tautology. Of course, this kind of basic thinking will upset those who hold that God commands, directs and inspires a defined code of morality. No, human customs are adopted, adapted and rejected based on whether they work or not. This is how we progress; we throw off customs, mores, that are no longer helpful or progressive, and we keep and modify those customs (ethics) that contribute to humankind's growth, happiness, progress. For good and for ill, customs change; and some customs change extremely slowly because of powerful interests vested in the past.

What if we Americans tossed off some of the most customary superstitions?

BETTER TAX LEGISLATION

For an important beginning, the phrase "honest politician" would be less likely an oxymoron; we would have many more honest politicians. If politicians no longer depended on the powerful pulpits of the Godly, these politicians could more reasonably vote their consciences. Of course, politicians are naturally beholden to many natural interest groups as well as to religious groups, but it seems to me that the supernatural groups (because of the size of their megaphones) get far more real benefits from pluralistic taxpaying society than they contribute back to that society.

In nearly every town and city in the country, some of the most valuable real estate would be added to the local tax base—not only the valuable corners where the churches sit but also their cemeteries, their generally unproductive parking lots, and the apartments and residences of related personnel. This one conformity with the Constitution would go far toward providing more adequate community services with balanced local budgets. Do the math; figure it out for your own community. You will likely be surprised, if not shocked, at just how serious this one violation of the First Amendment really is. Balanced budgets with lower tax rates can happen, without God or superstition.

A similar violation of the First Amendment is forced onto the general public by the income-tax code. The most glorious and ego-aggrandizing churches, cathedrals, synagogues, temples and mosques are bought or built and maintained with income-tax-exempt funds. This is clearly taxing everyone to subsidize these monuments to divisions in our society. The majority's tax bills are higher, because the donors of funds to build these buildings do not pay their fair share of taxes.

Taxes need to be collected for many obvious reasons. It is currently impossible, however, to know what our fair tax rates would be if religious organizations and their contributors were taxed as the rest of us. Without the unlikely cooperation of the churches themselves, no one can furnish even approximately reliable figures on the total church assets and annual income of the over 4,000 U.S. religions.

Back in 1997 (more recent figures not available), the Mormon Church's assets were found to be worth about thirty billion dollars. That church's annual income was then over six billion dollars (more than the whole budget of the State of Utah). Recognizing that Mormonism is only about the sixth largest religious group in U.S., you can see I'm not referring to just a few billions of overlooked tax dollars.

The assets and annual income of the U.S. Catholic Church, for example, dwarf those of the Mormons. The Catholic Church and its dioceses will not ever allow adequate auditing of the Church's financial books. So American taxpayers will never be able to determine what would be the fairly distributed tax burden as long religions are tax-exempt.

Religious charities do some obvious short-term good for society; and such good works hook a lot of dependent people. However, local social services, run as publicly subsidized and fully accountable (auditable) businesses, could do the job more professionally and more adequately. Such reason-based businesses, in open competition with each other, would ideally replace the faith-based businesses that fail to get the public scrutiny they deserve.

These reason-based businesses certainly should not and hopefully would not mix guilt-inducing proselytizing with their essential lessons on personal responsibility. Contrary to what Christ taught, poverty is not really necessary in the U.S., though it does seem to be unavoidable in the theocratic Middle East where all the three great Abrahamic religions originated and still compete with one another.

INCREASED PERSONAL RESPONSIBILITY

A benefit much greater than that of lower taxes would be the heightened sense of personal responsibility in our citizens. Briefly picture what life would be like if no one attributed human actions to God or Devil. There would be far less excuse making, whining, and "yes, butting." "Yes, I know I should help my neighborhood, but I am too poor; I didn't get the breaks the rich got. Yes, I ought to quit bingeing, but I had fat parents; I got bad genes. Devil made me do it. It may be the will of God; God works in mysterious ways. I was born this way; I can't help it. Shit happens!" With no God to throw the work to, I think loads of sniveling would disappear in a society of reasonably friendly and responsible citizens who say, "Life's not perfect, but we can make it better as we respectfully help each other."

What would happen to all those twelve-step therapy programs that to the naïve seem to be so helpful? Too often these programs, calling on some Power Higher than one's own personal power, furnish the addict with another excuse for ducking his own responsibility. Historically, many of these dependency-engendering twelve-step programs simplistically escort the devotees from one addiction to another, more religious dependency. A non-theistic or natural program of friendly mutual support would more effectively replace child-like sniveling and excuse-making with self-esteem and responsible independence. What a large leap forward this would be for the country!

DEEPER SENSE OF UNITY AMONG OUR CITIZENS

A huge leap forward would immediately result from having no competitive societal divisions based on whose religion is better or more true. Of course, we cannot have just one unifying religion; if we did, which one religion would it be? "United we stand," would no longer be so pervasively undermined by competing cults and religions in a non-theistic or truly secular and non-superstitious United States.

No one would come to your door to try to convert you to their way or entice you to read their "good books." You could talk reasonably about any topic (without excluding sex, religion and politics). Our politicians, now perhaps statesmen(?), could talk more reasonably to their rational constituencies. Non-superstitious rationalism would help both citizens and their representatives to think together rather than believe separately and divisively. We could stand united by reason! Such a life is but a dream until ... when?

U.S. WOULD BE AND SEEM MORE FRIENDLY TO OTHER NATIONS

Our self-defensive military budget would not consume such an irrationally large portion of our national budget if we tried to make friends rather than converts of other nations. We should have learned from Moses' mistake regarding neighbor relations that it is so much easier to negotiate honestly when there is no supernatural axe to grind. When it's just land, not holy land, argued about, compromise is easier and bloodshed less likely. Besides reducing our defense budget, our offensive military budget would be greatly reduced to become much less offensive. Eliminating the unconstitutional Chaplains Corps altogether would further reduce waste in the military budget.

Here's a really revolutionary suggestion: What if the U.S. admitted rationally that we cannot possibly defend against terrorism by force and still preserve our open, pluralistic society? Then could we afford a top-flight teachers corps, pay those teachers very well, and arm them with factual textbooks for the countries that currently hate America for appearing so aggressive, so force-and-fear-driven? This would not kill those "guilty" of disagreeing with us, but it surely would reduce their growing numbers—and for the pittance cost of only a few planes and their bombs!! Call it the war prevention program and pay for it with far less than one-thousandth of the military budget needed to rule by force and fear. Yes, of course, I know this is unrealistic with current religio-political "thinking"! Even if we are still a superpower, is it really necessary or helpful to act as some Moses-like divine avenger and destroy all those "evil" ones who believe or think differently?

IMPROVED PARENTAL AND
EDUCATIONAL EFFECTIVENESS

If United States parents and parental figures, in general, spent as much time teaching their children scientific facts as is wasted praying with or for them, they could all improve their productivity and security. In a 2002 National Science Foundation survey, over half of Americans said they believe in extrasensory perception and psychic powers. About as many believe in ghosts, communication with the dead, and lucky numbers. And, hard to believe, that same NSF survey found that half of Americans believe that man existed with the dinosaurs (an error of some 65 million years). I think a little more time needs to be spent on science education! Might want to add in some history, too, if you have the time.

GROSSLY IMPROVED FUNCTIONING
OF OUR JUSTICE SYSTEM

Yet another blessing of non-theism or atheism for American society could be immense. What if our justice system were so nonreligious that Old Testament type of vengeful punishment of criminals were not necessary? What if judges judged reasonably instead of doing the biblical eye-for-an-eye bit for criminals? Our extremely sick justice system now insists that punishment must fit the crime. Reasoned consequences or responsible restitution is really what should fit the crime, not punishment as such. Taxpayers cough up over $30,000 per year per criminal in prison, violent or not; this exceeds the annual cost of education at most of our excellent universities. We can design and execute really effective probation programs for far less!

What if criminals were sentenced according to their ability to be responsible and pay back, make restitution to society in accordance with their offense against society? Violent criminals would stay in jail to protect society, *not* to punish them. Non-violent criminals, under regular and thoughtful probationary supervision, would work to heal the society they wounded; they would pay back to society according to their talents and financial ability.

I think it is generally irrational and it should be considered immoral to imprison smart, non-violent people like Martha Stewart and those truly major criminals that destroyed Enron, Worldcom, Global Crossing and Tyco, in order to punish them. "Vengeance is mine, says the Lord!" Please let the Lord punish them! Don't punish or fine already wounded society by taxing society further to house the non-violent who do cooperate with rational and effective probation programs. Just because it would take some serious and extended thought to develop effective reason-based probation programs does not excuse us from developing same. Why should the above-referenced talented white-collar criminals be housed by society when they could be effectively depositing millions of dollars every Saturday into the coffers of their local probation programs? The basic reason is primarily punishment. And what does punishment as such profit society?

Some of these non-violent executives hurt millions of citizens. Why not fine them very, very heavily for the stolen millions or billions, the fines of restitution (plus collection costs) to be paid off weekly and *in person* to the responsible legal authorities? It's utterly and inexcusably stupid and wasteful to bury such talent in jail, then bill the working taxpayer for their prison expenses (or their extensive prison-avoiding legal expenses). Such punishment shows an outdated, Old Testament religious concept that further punishes an already wounded society!

Non-violent blue-collar criminals could work at their jobs to earn competitive or union scale pay, likewise under responsible probationary supervision. They, too, turn in their fines weekly by way of restitution to the community or families they wounded. Non-violent criminals stay out of jail as long as they obey the strict and productive terms of their probation. When will we learn that it is very difficult to punish productively? This vengeful punishment is an idea from Mosaic times and based on an assumed God who named himself "Jealous." The Bible has God saying, "Vengeance is mine; I will repay." Let God grab all the vengeance he can; a thoughtful, unsuperstitious society needs restitution, not vengeance.

Firm and reliable consequences for irresponsible behavior are essential to an intelligent justice system. Punishment commonly causes counterproductive anger that deepens the anti-social tendencies in the criminal. I don't think it's reasonable to keep well over 2,000,000 Americans (almost one percent of our citizens) behind bars when less than 30% of those prisoners are violent threats to society (*Time Almanac 2000*). Punish, punish, punish; punish whom? Already injured society!

No, I am not going soft on crime. As a psychologist, I know that the death penalty (I prefer "the death consequence") is very under-utilized, and, yes, contrary to a lot of doctored and biased "research reports," it is a definite deterrent from crime! The next time you see any sort of "research report" that concludes that the death consequence does not deter, check both the authorship and the assumptions of such a report. With only rare exceptions, a person's strongest drive is to continue living. How can such a basic fact be ignored by so many?

A life sentence without possibility of parole for the non-violent criminal is generally ludicrous. It punishes the criminal endlessly while it expensively punishes the society that has already been hurt by the criminal. The death consequence, for those and **only** those who are **certainly** responsible for the most heinous crimes, is often far more appropriate than such outrageous sentences. *Never* should a doubtfully guilty person be executed; but with the help of DNA testing, many of the old doubts can be set aside. At the very least, the violent criminal under such a silly sentence as "life without parole" should be able to choose the death consequence as an option. "But, no, only God can take a life." Baloney! Did God kill the drunk driver crashing into the concrete wall?

Such an illogical stance is about as outrageous as the 2006 case of California murderer Clarence Allen. He had been scheduled for execution, but at 75, legally blind and nearly deaf, his attorneys appealed for a stay of execution all the way to the U.S.

Supreme Court. And what was the appeal based on? Not that he was innocent, not that he did not deserve to be put to death, but the appeal was based on fact that if the state were to put such an ill old man to death, it would be cruel and unusual punishment! Do you think his appeal lawyers were doing their work *pro bono*, or is it much more likely that they were getting paid well for such ludicrous appeal efforts?

Our religiously vengeful politicians, reflecting the attitudes of their constituencies, over-legislate and micro-manage our justice system more and more, and their lawyer friends capitalize on it handsomely. As a result, punishment of the criminal continues to grow in importance. One frightening result is that good judges find they are impotent to use good judgment, get discouraged, retire early and leave the judges' benches to the more politically correct judges. Retiring U.S. district judge, John S. Martin, Jr., wrote in *The New York Times* (2003): "When I took my oath of office 13 years ago, I never thought I would leave the federal bench. While I might have stayed on despite the inadequate pay, I no longer want to be part of our unjust criminal justice system."

I am barely scratching the surface of this truly immense American problem of crime and vengeful punishment. But can you already see that many billions of tax dollars could be saved annually if vengeful religious-type punishment-of-the-wicked were thoughtfully removed from all our penal codes? Would "Codes of Consequences" be far better than "Penal Codes"? If the outdated concept of punishment as such were removed from our justice system and if a system of fair consequences were firmly followed, I doubt it would be necessary to lock up about one percent of our population as we do now.

In summary, without superstition life in the United States could improve the observance of the First Amendment, reduce taxes, increase personal responsibility, deepen unity among U.S. and world citizens, improve educational efforts, and vastly improve our justice system.

This litany represents a mere handful of the potential improvements that could result from having a truly non-theistic or atheistic American society. Though there are many other advantages of a reasoned approach to life over a religious or faith-based approach, it is currently unrealistic to expect the United States to quickly become an atheistic or non-theistic society, even though our Constitution does not argue against it. Too many politicians and lawyers have interests vested in powerful pulpits that have vested interests in politicians to allow such humanistic atheism. Society has to evolve and mature a great deal more and appreciate The Golden Rule far more than it does now before reason can reign as our highest power.

SEQUITUR/NON SEQUITUR— "I LOVE THIS PLANET HERE"

That rousing song by the agnostic, Irving Berlin, *God Bless America*, learned in my days of faith, still stirs this author's heart. Now, though, it is an impure pleasure for me to sing it lustily with fellow Americans. It would be a pure pleasure, indeed, to sing the following lyrics to that familiar Berlin melody:

> While old hates lighten, for both you and me
> We now show affection, for a land so free.
> We can all be helpful; this is really home
> With The Gold'n Rule, wherever we roam.
>
> I love this planet here, land of our home.
> Don't divide it, help unite it
> By a life that is right full of love.
> Bring your talents to your neighbors,
> For more friendship, warmed with love.
> I love this planet here, land of our home.
> I love this planet here, land of our home.

TEN

THE GOLDEN RULE

THE GOLDEN RULE WITHOUT SUPERSTITION

Surely the most basic of general guidelines for getting along in society is The Golden Rule: "Treat others as you would reasonably want and expect them to treat you if your roles were reversed." This important guide for human happiness and productivity is quite common-sensical and, therefore, has a long history. That is, The Golden Rule has a long history of being preached; its history of reasonable implementation is much more limited.

GOLDEN RULE OF PRE-CHRISTIAN ORIGIN

I used to believe this important guide originated with Christ; that, along with a lot of my earlier beliefs, is not true. The Golden Rule can be found among the many contradictory laws of Jewish tradition earlier than 1200 B.P.E.: "Do not seek revenge or bear grudge against one of your people, but love your neighbor as yourself..." (Lev. 19:18) Then a contradictory commandment that sounds like The Golden Rule with vengeance creeps into Leviticus only five short chapters later: "If anyone injures his neighbor, whatever he has done must be done to him: fracture for fracture, eye for eye, tooth for tooth. As he has injured the other, so he is to be injured." (Lev. 24:19-20) Vengeful punishment overrides neighborly love very frequently in this biblical tradition.

The Chinese tradition, reflected by Confucius (sixth century B.P.E.), taught The Golden Rule in an improved fashion: "Do not do to another what you would not want done to you." Then almost six centuries later, Christ said: "So in everything, do to others what you would have them do to you, for this sums up the Law and the Prophets." (Mt. 7:12) Any informed Bible student can tell you this rule does not sum up most of the Law and the Prophets, though it certainly does far excel most of the Law and the Prophets.

What is helpful here is to realize the long tradition of respect for the common sense or reasonable notion of what has come to be called The Golden Rule. It is very helpful to understand that this most rational directive has no divine origin. A clear-thinking person can see The Golden Rule as most helpful for good social (as well as business) relationships. And since good social relationships pay off so well for the well-adjusted, The Golden Rule could be called the universal law for social welfare or the great guide for truly enlightened selfishness.

Since it is no longer necessary nor helpful to assume there is a God of some sort, what follows? Since nothing follows this life, we must surely do our reasonable best to make this the best life we can make it. If we are to make it the best possible for ourselves, we must also help to make it better for those around us—the rest of humankind—our global neighbors. Enlightened selfishness drives us to help others enjoy a better life. Make friends, not converts!

When a neighbor is happier, the neighborhood is happier. If we help a neighbor, we help ourselves. Reasonable generosity may look like selflessness; I would rather call it enlightened selfishness. This concept of enlightened selfishness may offend some, but it's love beginning at home and not staying there. The intelligently selfish person helps his neighbor, his neighbor more likely helps others, and (either directly or indirectly) those others are also more likely to help the original intelligently selfish person. This enlightened selfishness is the secret to happy marriages and constitutes virtuous cycles of generosity. Certainly no supernatural wisdom is needed to see this.

ENLIGHTENED SELFISHNESS CALLS FOR THE GOLDEN RULE

If you help others get more out of life, so will you get more out of life. If you both secretly and publicly work to help your spouse or significant other to benefit, you will have a happier relationship; if you secretly and publicly smooth a neighbor's path toward success and happiness, you will live in a happier, more successful community. I don't care if your act of help is as small as picking up a carelessly dropped paper towel from a public washroom floor, or as big as mentoring a neglected child. You will generally gain at several levels if you make the world a little better for your having been here.

Families make up neighborhoods. Neighborhoods make up the world! Wherever you go, once in a while do a little bit to make your and your neighbor's world at least a little bit better. Don't expect praise or pay. The praise may never come; the pay will almost always come. If, for example, you generously or cooperatively let another driver enter traffic in front of you, your effort will make someone less angry, less cynical, more hopeful, more positive and, therefore, more helpful; then that person is more likely to be cooperative and generous with some other fellow human being, "and the world will be better for this." Besides, it feels good; it's reasonable; it is *not* "The Impossible Dream."

Since the reasonable non-believer or secular humanist does not hope for heaven in an imaginary world beyond this life, he generously works more sincerely to make this real world a place of peace, joy and opportunity. In the words of that great lady and fine actress, Katherine Hepburn: "I am an atheist; I believe there is nothing we can know except that we should be kind to each other and do what we can for other people." When this really bright star died June 29, 2003, both television and the printed media were generous with their accolades, expressing great admiration for her excellent acting ability, inner strength and independence. However, I failed to find even one single mention of her deeply held convictions regarding the central importance of The Golden Rule and her atheism. How regrettable that we have such biased, incomplete and superficial reporting of important facts.

If we thinking human beings demonstrate The Golden Rule as enthusiastically as the credulous and superstitious manipulators push the opiate of the dream world, we will have fewer dependent addicts among us! It should be easy, natural and reasonable for the thinking person to treat a fellow human being as he would reasonably want and expect to be treated if the roles were reversed. It's the natural way for mutually respectful love to begin at home and spread through neighborhoods and the rest of humankind.

AMERICA PROFITS BY THE GOLDEN RULE

Perhaps the greatest good to come out of the horrible faith-based tragedy of 9/11/01 will be the growing realization that theocracies or superstition-based governments rule by dogmatic dictates rather than by democratic or mutual understanding between the government and the governed. When divinely revealed theocratic dictates are challenged, terror is used to force compliance. So beware of the dogma. Such governments, under God, tend to collapse after briefly lording artificial authority over the governed, because "power corrupts, and absolute power corrupts absolutely." By contrast, successful democracies demonstrate The Golden Rule of mutual respect between the government and the governed.

It is no accident that the U.S. Constitution is atheistic; the founding fathers were very wise. They had seen the deadly and divisive little theocracies with their murders of "witches" and other severe punishments for religious non-conformity in the early new world colonies when majorities failed to respect minorities. Consequently, it is likewise no accident that our Constitution is the oldest democratic constitution in existence. It stands the tests of time, because it is reasonable, not divinely inspired nor divinely supported. In respecting and listening to its governed people, truly democratic government is far closer to The Golden Rule than an authoritarian, Moses-like dictatorship that sees authority as coming from above rather than from the give-and-take consent of the governed.

We atheists, agnostics, skeptics, rationalists, humanists, secularists, naturalists of various stripes respect each other and get along with our fellow human beings reasonably well. We know the value of The Golden Rule from reason. And we appear to observe it more consistently than the members of warring religious sects and dogmatic governments. We can be proud of the fact that we do not make violent headlines revealing crimes against our fellow human beings, young and old.

We non-theists made up fourteen percent of the U.S. population in 2001, when self-proclaimed religious patriots and politicians thought we should still be ignored. However, less than ten years earlier, this fourteen percent had been only eight percent. So our U.S. numbers increased seventy-five percent in ten years. During the same decade of the 1990s, the Mormons, the fastest growing religion in the United States, increased by less than twenty percent.

Though the non-religious population has shown an impressively rapid growth rate, I fear it is not fast enough to stop the rapid destruction of the Wall of Separation between Church and State. This is no idle fear, for already in 2002 an office of religion was established in our White House itself. If you are tempted to minimize the importance of such a move, I urge you to read an impressive little book by Frederick Clarkson, *Eternal Hostility*, to see how effectively the real attackers of the Church/State wall are flying below the radar of the popular press.

For thinkers to counterbalance the credulous, we fourteen percent (and growing rapidly) need to increase our influence. In the Dark Ages of Faith, it was hard to convince humankind that the earth was not flat; it will now be difficult to convince deeply entrenched vested interests that The Golden Rule can become humankind's guideline *without* the need for religion or superstition.

We need to show more consistently that once we drop the myth of Original Sin that declares that all of us are born sinful, bad and weak, the crutch of religion and superstition is no longer needed. Without guilt, who needs redemption? As the body of human knowledge increases, humankind is gradually getting more and more reasonable. Though progress toward the universal acceptance of the natural wisdom of The Golden Rule may seem slow, it is real progress that will never be stopped.

Honest Abe Lincoln got it right in saying, you can fool some of the people all the time and all of the people some of the time; but you can't fool all the people all the time. The California lawmakers got it right in 2002 when their legislation endorsed stem cell research in spite of the obstructive objection of believers in Washington, D.C. Even though right-wingers grow bolder in their desperate attacks, more and more perceptive people are noticing that the Divine Emperor has no clothes at all, that the God assumption is groundless, that eating of the Tree of Knowledge is good, that natural truth will make you free.

The rate of rational progress toward universal and natural observance of The Golden Rule seems slow; the majority still clings to old ways while the attackers of the Jeffersonian wall grow bolder. The reasoned application of The Golden Rule in all your dealings will attract reliable friends of good humanity, voters as well as non-voters who yearn to be free of manipulative lies and politically correct hypocrisy. Fewer and fewer people will choose to be fooled by the hellish threats and empty promises of an impotent God.

I foresee, for the coming information-based generation of

bio-technologists, neurobiologists, embryologists, nanotechnologists, stem cell researchers, microfluidics experts, space travelers, etc., a new birth of friendly freedom based on The Golden Rule. This exciting development will gradually gain speed as human knowledge continues to grow at an ever quickening pace, as this marvelous human race gets more and more comfortable in the shade of the Tree of Knowledge.

Let your neighbors know that you are a helpful, generous, friendly, rational optimist; show that you are *not a cynic* who contends that The Golden Rule means that he who has the gold gets to rule. And certainly show by your political involvement that you emphatically reject the popular political posture that The Golden Rule means that he who rules gets the gold! Politicians will finally start to notice when more and more of us demonstrate natural goodness and generosity by, for examples, working for better science courses in our schools, sponsoring and helping with environmental clean-ups, helping the deserving poor and desperate, mentoring and volunteering privately and publicly where needed to make our local world a little bit better.

The Golden Rule according to Confucius remains as reasonable and practical for us today as it was half a millennium B.P.E.: "Don't treat another in a way you would not want to be treated!" If we consistently and reasonably observe this Golden Rule, we non-believers, non-credulous, in the U.S. population will quickly attract another fourteen percent of the thinking population. We can show the world that reason-based democracy is the most practical way for all of us relatives in the human family to bring ourselves together in productive, peaceful, rational, mutually supportive relationships. *E pluribus unum* (from many one, from many colonies one country, from many countries one world, from many races one humanity)!

SEQUITUR/NON SEQUITUR—
RELIGIOUS INTOLERANCE

As I was walking across a high bridge, I saw a man standing on the edge. He was about to jump, so I ran over and said, "Stop! Don't do it!"

"Why shouldn't I?" he asked.

I said, "Well, there's so much to live for!"

"Like what?" he asked.

"Well," I asked, "are you religious or atheist?"

He said, "Religious."

I said, "Me too! Are you Christian or Buddhist?"

He said, "Christian."

"Me too," I said. "Are you Catholic or Protestant?"

He said, "Protestant."

I said, "Me too. Are you Episcopalian or Baptist?"

He said, "Baptist."

I said, "Wow! Me too! Are you Baptist Church of God or Baptist Church of the Lord?"

He said, "Baptist Church of God."

I said, "Me too! Are you Original Baptist Church of God, or are you Reformed Baptist Church of God?"

He said, "Reformed Baptist Church of God!"

I said, "Me too! Are you Reformed Baptist Church of God, Reformation of 1879, or Reformed Baptist Church of God, Reformation of 1915?"

He said, "Reformed Baptist Church of God, Reformation of 1915!"

I said, "Die, heretic scum!" and pushed him off.

ELEVEN

TEN COMMANDMENTS FOR THE TWENTY-FIRST CENTURY

These are ten commandments that can be posted, taught, and observed anywhere without violating conscience or Constitution:

1. First, treat others as you would reasonably want and expect to be treated if your roles were reversed. (This first commandment makes all the others easier.)
2. Never bear false witness to the young and credulous.
3. Do not pass on traditional myths, manipulations and superstitions as cultural heritage.
4. Never imply to the young or naïve that you know what you do not know; they will respect you much longer.

5. Admit that in nature there are no mysteries, just temporary ignorance of natural facts.
6. Study and work with discipline to learn and then teach the great, beautiful, amazing scientific facts of nature.
7. Enjoy helping the younger generation excel beyond their ancestors as they stand on your reliable shoulders.
8. Do not be afraid of the truth learned in gentle, consistent, rational discipline; it will make both you and your students responsibly free.
9. Teach your youngsters to use every available scientific tool to appreciate all of the real world.
10. When you offer your shoulders for youngsters to stand on, be very careful not to face backward towards the darkness of the superstitious past, but rather forward toward the light of their future.

* * *

These ten simple guidelines can help you make our world better for your having lived in it. Enjoy **this** life deeply!

EPILOGUE

For many years I have lived in joyful harmony with my closest neighbor, my wife, who has always known that I had been a Catholic priest-become-atheist; I did not deceive her in this regard. We have successfully stayed good friends as we have worked to help each other to benefit. This is the most practical basis of good relationships, because it demonstrates The Golden Rule.

I thought it practical to keep most of my other neighbors and friends in the dark regarding my clerical background, even while working generously in our little community to help them to benefit. So far, this has worked beautifully; great neighbor relations and good friendships have developed; we neighbors and friends have helped each other to benefit—again showing that The Golden Rule really does work.

Now that I have "come out of the closet," I hope that none of these caring relationships will be threatened by the fact that my conscience has driven me far beyond my old belief systems. We all develop at different rates according to our very personal insights and experiences; I fondly hope that these differences will not divide us but will further unite us as we thoughtfully tolerate each other's different insights and developmental rates. Then we will continue helping each other to benefit.

Can you, will you now help others in your family, social, business and political networks to come **Out of God's Closet?** Will you show them the joy of true friendship on our shrinking pluralistic planet? As neighborhoods benefit, this world gets better. The practical wisdom of The Golden Rule is really much more precious than gold. That is why the profits from this book are being donated to charity—**that we all may be one.**

Thank you sincerely,
Stephen F. Uhl
www.OutOfGodsCloset.com

....

Now help at least three other persons, bookstores or organizations to enjoy life more richly by sharing:

Retail or wholesale, save both time and money as you --

ORDER DIRECTLY from: The Friendly Order Desk
Publishers Express Press
200 West 5th Street South
P.O. Box 123
Ladysmith, WI 54848
(715) 532-5300
(800) 255-9929
FAX (715) 532-4888
email: pubexpress@centurytel.net
Visa, MasterCard and Discover Cards accepted.

"... and the world will be better for this ..."

Now is the **best** time to make our world better!

APPENDIX I

Sincere thanks to professor Paul Kurtz as well as The Council for Secular humanism for allowing the re-printing of the following **Affirmations of Humanism**, which spell out so well the ethics of The Golden Rule for modern humankind:

THE AFFIRMATIONS OF HUMANISM

A STATEMENT OF PRINCIPLES
By
Prof. Paul Kurtz, Ph.D.

We are committed to the application of reason and science to the understanding of the universe and to the solving of human problems.

We deplore efforts to denigrate human intelligence, to seek to explain the world in supernatural terms, and to look outside nature for salvation.

We believe that scientific discovery and technology can contribute to the betterment of human life.

We believe in an open and pluralistic society and that democracy is the best guarantee of protecting human rights from authoritarian elites and repressive majorities.

We are committed to the principle of the separation of church and state.

We cultivate the arts of negotiation and compromise as a means of resolving differences and achieving mutual understanding.

We are concerned with securing justice and fairness in society and with eliminating discrimination and intolerance.

We believe in supporting the disadvantaged and the handicapped so that they will be able to help themselves.

We attempt to transcend divisive parochial loyalties based on race, religion, gender, nationality, creed, class, sexual orientation, or ethnicity, and strive to work together for the common good of humanity.

We want to protect and enhance the earth, to preserve it for future generations, and to avoid inflicting needless suffering on other species.

We believe in enjoying life here and now and developing our creative talents to their fullest.

We believe in the cultivation of moral excellence.

We respect the right to privacy. Mature adults should be allowed to fulfill their aspirations, to express their sexual preferences, to exercise reproductive freedom, to have access to comprehensive and informed health-care, and to die with dignity.

We believe in the common moral decencies: altruism, integrity, honesty, truthfulness, responsibility. Humanist ethics is amenable to critical, rational guidance. There are normative standards that we discover together. Moral principles are tested by their consequences.

We are deeply concerned with the moral education of our children. We want to nourish reason and compassion.

We are engaged by the arts no less than by the sciences.

We are citizens of the universe and are excited by discoveries still to be made in the cosmos.

We are skeptical of untested claims to knowledge, and we are open to novel ideas and seek new departures in our thinking.

We affirm humanism as a realistic alternative to theologies of despair and ideologies of violence and as a source of rich personal significance and genuine satisfaction in the service of others.

We believe in optimism rather than pessimism, hope rather than despair, learning in the place of dogma, truth instead of ignorance, joy rather than guilt or sin, tolerance in the place of fear, love instead of hatred, compassion over selfishness, beauty instead of ugliness, and reason rather than blind faith or irrationality.

We believe in the fullest realization of the best and noblest that we are capable of as human beings.

(http://www.secularhumanism.org)

APPENDIX II

A DECLARATION OF
PROGRESSIVE PRINCIPLES

(Special thanks to Larry A. Sakin, Coordinator of The Principles Project, for allowing inclusion here of the truly progressive principles showing how The Golden Rule should be lived in social and political life.)

We believe in America's historic promise of liberty, justice and the expansion of opportunity for all people. These commitments to fundamental human dignity and a better nation for all animate the American spirit and give us a sense of common purpose. We honor these commitments by recognizing that with the great freedoms afforded us comes an even greater responsibility to see that those freedoms are extended to all people in all places.

We believe that this sense of shared responsibility—for our

families, our communities, our nation and our world—strengthens our country and secures our future.

* * *

We believe in defending dignity:

"All people are created equal" is not just a fact—it is a call to action. Either we create justice for all or we have justice for none.

All people have the right to lead their personal lives in accordance with their own beliefs, free from imposition or monitoring by others.

All people have a right to the basic necessities required to lead dignified lives and to pursue happiness.

We believe in strengthening democracy:

It is the shared responsibility of a nation to ensure each citizen's freedom, security and equality. Through government, we honor our responsibility to promote the common good.

Government must be transparent, accessible and open to all citizens who wish to oversee its working and share in its benefits.

America must work to enhance the democratic process by ensuring an educated citizenry, equal opportunity for influence, honest public debate, competitive elections and robust civic participation.

A healthy democracy requires tireless vigilance against corruption and abuses of power, and a government that is accountable to its people.

We believe in promoting progress:

We must promote innovation and entrepreneurship, cultivate the arts and sciences, and ensure a quality education for everyone. When we invest in individual potential, the benefits are shared by all.

America must continue to be a welcoming home to all people.

We believe that diversity of faith, culture and perspective enriches our nation.

America must keep a watchful eye on the economy to ensure fairness, transparency and genuine opportunity for all.

Each generation has a duty to protect and improve those resources we hold in common—our community spaces, our public institutions and our natural environment.

We believe in embracing leadership:

America's security requires an effective military and a commitment to enduring alliances, but we must remember that America's true power is found in its wisdom as well as its strength.

Our security and prosperity rely on the security and prosperity of people throughout the world. By helping others, we will help ourselves.

America must join with other nations to build global institutions that protect the vulnerable, promote democratic self-government, and improve the health and welfare of all people throughout the world.

America must never suspend its belief in democracy and human rights in the pursuit of its global objectives. Noble ends require nothing short of noble means.

* * *

As progressives, these are our guiding principles—to defend dignity, to strengthen democracy, to promote progress and to embrace leadership. We believe that our country must always be looking toward a better and brighter future for all people, and in this pursuit we pledge to come forward and work with whomever we can. We will fight for these principles in every community, every forum and every office of government, because the struggles of this new century will not only be about preserving the freedoms we already enjoy—they will be about expanding those freedoms for all people.

(http://principlesproject.com)

SOME OF THE MANY HELPFUL HUMANISTIC GROUPS

A plethora of secular humanist or non-theistic groups function throughout the nation and the world. Such groups are ready, willing and able to help persons interested in experiencing more deeply what non-theism has to offer. The millions of secularists, rationalists, agnostics, atheists, humanists, and other non-theists have the opportunity for greater strength through cooperative unity.

If you or your group wants information or local support, you may choose to contact any of the groups on the following page via the internet:

1. Center For Inquiry
2. Council for Secular humanism
3. Americans United
4. Campus Freethought Alliance
5. American humanist Association
6. The Coalition for the Community of Reason
7. Secular Student Alliance
8. Committee for Skeptical Inquiry
9. Atheist Alliance International
10. Institute for Humanist Studies
11. Humanist Society of Friends
12. People For the American Way
13. International Humanist and Ethical Union
14. Camp Quest
15. North American Committee for Humanism
16. Freedom From Religion Foundation
17. Internet Infidels
18. College Democrats of America
19. Humanist Association of Canada
20. Freethought Association of Canada
21. Military Association of Atheists and Freethinkers
22. Society for Humanistic Judaism
23. International Humanist and Ethical Youth Organization
24. Rational Response Squad
25. American Atheists
26. EvolveFISH
27. The Secular Coalition for America

INDEX

SOME COMMENTS FROM THE READERS OF THE FIRST PRINTING OF *IMAGINE NO SUPERSTITION*.

So simple, clear and funny ... I couldn't put it down ... so profound I had to read it again.

Finally, self-help that is fundamentally and really helpful . ... Besides, it's funny!

This former priest-psychologist clearly knows the human heart.

Piercing, fearless, joyful, freeing, life changing, concise, practical, tolerant, insightful, funny, powerful, down-to-earth

Now I finally understand how prayer works.

I can't decide which deserves the greater kudos, Dr. Uhl's revised Golden Rule or The Ten Commandments for the 21st Century.

The beautiful "Declaration of Progressive Principles" shows well how The Golden Rule should be lived in social and political life.

"...profound and simple. Profound in that it deals with some of the most important concepts facing the world today, simple in that it is clear and persuasive. Dr. Uhl is able to speak from an unusual perspective. He is a former Roman Catholic priest and has moved very carefully and thoughtfully to an agnostic/atheist position. His insights are remarkable, ... (M)any of us who are increasingly doubtful about the existence of the supernatural ... will find the book a very solid grounding for our currently vague concerns. An excellent and thoughtful exposition of important and even crucial ideas."

Philip E. Johnson, Ph.D., Educator, Author

"Uhl correctly states that this book is not a scholarly work. He's right but that is part of its inherent value. He is able to understand, and describe, the intimate person as only a priest or psychologist can. His psychological expertise gives excellent insight into the human psyche while his in-depth ecclesiastical knowledge exposes the mechanisms and motives of the clergy. He does a superb job of intermixing personal experience, empirical data, linear reasoning, anecdotal stories, and sometimes outrageously humorous supporting material to project clear understanding. The result is a delightfully entertaining, informative and interesting work."

Michael Judge, Reviewer. Freethought Society of
Greater Philadelphia

"To say it is a memorable book would be the understatement of the year. I've ordered several copies to give to friends ... struggling with the idea of giving up on religion and superstitions in favor of common sense. It really is a superior book–the kind you can't read just once."

Ila Deluca, National Secretary Final Exit Network

"I finished ... your book ... and thought it was wonderful. I liked the way you wove little jokes into the main body of the work... I really loved it. Everyone who has managed to shuck off the bonds of superstition has a story to tell, but some people have a special flair for telling them. The fact that you were once a Catholic priest makes yours even more fascinating."

Catherine Fahringer, Writer Freethought Today

Hi, Stephen,

I finally had time to read your book, *Imagine No Superstition*. It's really terrific! I hope you sell a zillion copies! As an author myself (11 published books), I was very impressed with the professionalism of your book. Did you have it professionally copy edited, or are you just very skilled? I'm in awe!

Many thanks,

Susan Sackett—Writer, President of the Humanist Society of Greater Phoenix

"I read your book and was quite impressed that you were able to fit so many subjects into so few pages. It was an easy read and I don't disagree with anything in the book."

Mel Lipman, President American Humanist Association

"Why, oh why, was I so blind - - was it because I felt I didn't have the 'right to question'?

"I am so grateful to you for sharing 'your story' with all of us —your very candid and, at times, humorous remarks. It truly reinforces the reasons for change in my life."

Dean Myhr, Art Critic, Director Art Gallery

"After showing an impressive series of ways human life would be better without any superstitious mysteries or sectarian wars, this outstanding book concludes that nothing works as well for human freedom and happiness as the tolerant and completely natural Golden Rule... When one spouse makes the other look good, that caring love washes right back on the first spouse; when that caring family helps the neighbors, the neighbors help right back and the neighborhood improves for everyone. Such reasonable caring answers clearly the popular but shallow question: 'How can you be a good person if you don't believe in God?'

"*Out of God's Closet* is small in size but impressively powerful, grippingly interesting and a sorely needed read for our time."
Mary Jean Clements, de-converted grandmother
and housewife

Feel free to share your own "readers comments" at:
www.OutOfGodsCloset.com.

....

Now help at least three other persons, bookstores or organizations to
enjoy life more richly by sharing:

Retail or wholesale, save both time and money as you --

ORDER DIRECTLY from: The Friendly Order Desk
Publishers Express Press
200 West 5th Street South
P.O. Box 123
Ladysmith, WI 54848
(715) 532-5300
(800) 255-9929
FAX (715) 532-4888
email: pubexpress@centurytel.net

Visa, MasterCard and Discover Cards accepted.

"... and the world will be better for this ..."

Now is the **best** time to make our world better!